HART STRINGS

Paul Jay: "Are you looking forward to the day that Bret hangs up his boots?"

Julie Hart: "I've been waiting since the day he was twenty-five. It's been eighteen years now, and I'm sure it's always going to be the same."

Paul Jay: "But you've had enough."

Julie Hart: ". . . Yes. . . Yes, I have. . . I think it's time to be normal."

From the film *Wrestling with Shadows*,

directed by Paul Jay (1998, High Roads Production)

HART STRINGS

my life with Bret and The Hart Family

by Julie Hart

Tightrope Books Inc.
167 Browning Trail
Barrie, Ontario
Canada L4N 5E7
www.tightropebooks.com

Editors: Nathaniel G. Moore, Deanna Janovski
Copy Editor: Jessica Hale
Cover Design: Deanna Janovski
Typesetting: David Bigham

Produced with the support of the Canada Council for the Arts and the Ontario Arts Council

Canada Council for the Arts Conseil des Arts du Canada

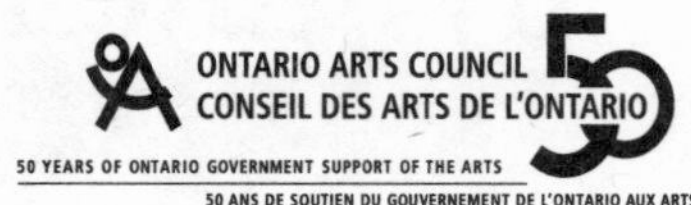

Library and Archives Canada Cataloguing in Publication

Hart, Julie
Hart strings / Julie Hart.

ISBN 978-1-926639-63-5

1. Hart, Julie. 2. Hart, Bret. 3. Hart family. 4. Wrestlers' Spouses--Alberta--Calgary--Biography. 5. Wrestlers--Alberta--Calgary--Biography. I. Title.

Printed in Canada

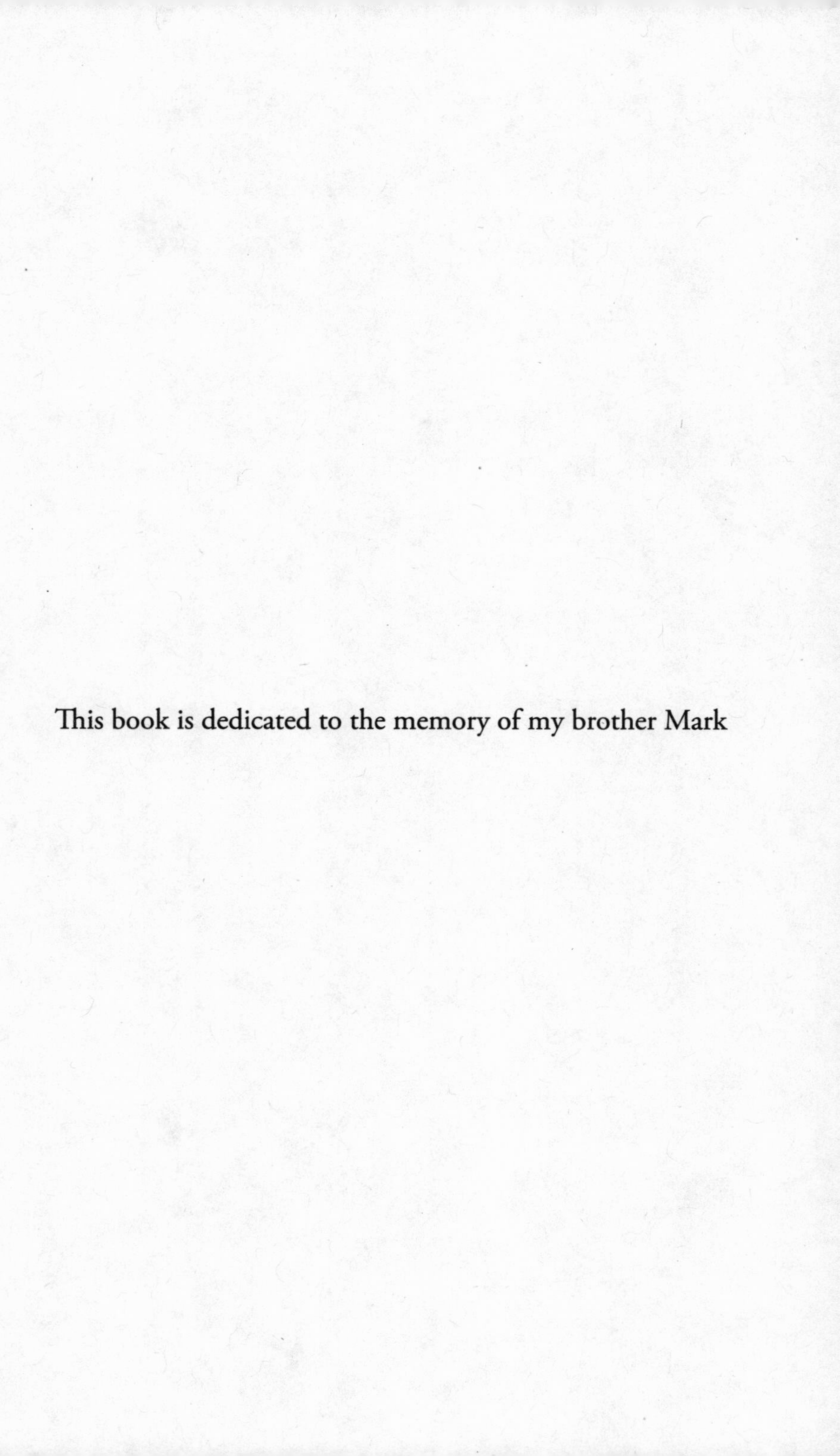

This book is dedicated to the memory of my brother Mark

Contents

A glooming peace this morning with it brings;
The sun, for sorrow, will not show his head:
Go hence, to have more talk of these sad things;
Some shall be pardon'd, and some punished:
For never was a story of more woe
Than this of Juliet and her Romeo.

Romeo & Juliet, William Shakespeare

Prologue: *Romeo and Juliet*

In the spring of 1996, Bret called from South Africa, where he was filming *Sinbad*, to ask if I wanted to come see him. He had been there for a couple of weeks and sounded lonely. I was thrilled he wanted me to come, as we hadn't been getting along so well. He kept telling me how amazing it was there, and that I needed to see it for myself. He'd made friends with some really cool people and said they would take great care of us. The cast was really friendly, especially this guy Robin, who had become a buddy of Bret's. Bret said Robin was huge and would be perfect for the WWF. He told me to book a babysitter; he'd take care of the rest.

I asked our friend Wanda if she would watch the kids for a couple of weeks, and she said no problem. Bret called back to tell me he'd booked a bed and breakfast for us. He reminded me to pack warm clothes because they were just getting out of winter there and it would be a bit chilly. Funny, but I pictured Africa as a desert with people in saris. I thought of safaris and people with staffs roaming about with their thin little animals. My ignorance was sometimes surprising to Bret. When I brought up my vision of Africa, he quickly corrected me: "Jules, that's farther up, this is the white part of Africa, settled by the Dutch. Apartheid happened here. Anyway, you're going to love it here, Crabby, it's beautiful."

Bret always kept himself informed about all the places he went to. That was no surprise. I, on the other hand, felt dumb. I was never really interested in the political histories of countries. That stuff bored me. But I made an effort to find out more this time, if only to get a sense of what the country offered. I eagerly searched online for things to do, mostly typical tourist things. Bret had everything planned out for us, but I still wanted to be in charge of what I wanted to see. I knew I would be spending a lot of downtime on my own while Bret was filming. I made myself a list of places I wanted to visit. At the top of that list was a library that housed a facsimile of Shakespeare's first folio. I'd seen some amazing things overseas with Bret, but I felt like this would outdo them all.

I fell in love with *Romeo and Juliet* while taking high school equivalency classes in the early 1990s. Most of the students struggled with Shakespeare, but I took to it right away. I felt like I instantly understood exactly what they were saying, even though I'd never studied Shakespeare before. I chalked it up to a past life. Perhaps I had once lived in the Elizabethan era.

I scurried about the rest of the week, getting ready for the trip. I was quite a pudgy little mouse of a wife and was anxious about being around beautiful Dutch women and Bret's actress friends. I was also worried about not being able to smoke with Bret around. I had picked up the habit again, and on top of that, I was still popping Prozac. The night before I left, Bret called to remind me to bring some Halcion along for the fourteen-hour flight to Cape Town. I hated taking them when he wasn't with me. I often lost control of myself while on those little pills. Without Bret there to keep an eye on me and block me in, I was liable to get up in a haze and do silly things. It was just more anxiety to add to the heaping pile of shit that was already running through my head.

I was going through a dark time in my life. My self-esteem was at an all-time low and nothing was making me happy anymore. According to my therapist, I was engaging in complete self-sabotage. I had been making myself scarce and hiding from everybody. I felt like it was a terrible time for me to be going on a trip, but in my heart I really wanted to make this trip fun and have a good time with Bret. I was hoping we would get some alone time to figure things out between us. As I flew over the Atlantic and stared out the tiny window, I vowed to make things better for Bret and myself.

When I landed in Cape Town, I was more excited about seeing Shakespeare's folio than Bret. I gave Bret a hug and was whisked off to the set of *Sinbad*, even though I was horribly tired and not that interested in seeing it. Bret scolded me when I told him I hadn't taken the sleeping pills. He went on about how important it was to get adjusted to the time zone. I snapped back that jet lag was never a problem for me. So it began.

I was introduced to the cast of *Sinbad*, who were all very nice. I especially liked Bret's friend Robin. He was loud and jovial, and he smoked, which was great for me. We sat around chatting and marveling at the landscape while Bret did his scenes, and when Bret was done, Robin invited us over for dinner. In a charming accent that sounded slightly English, Robin said that it wouldn't be a gourmet meal, but "something to put in the belly 'til morn."

It was quite dark when we got to Robin's. I excused myself for a moment, hoping to get in a quick smoke. Robin warned me not to stray too far—there were terrible things that could gallop off with me. I decided it was worth the risk for a quick drag. Outside, the sounds were unlike anything I'd ever heard before. It was so much more than the chirping of crickets or croaking of frogs; it was like a choir of insects in unison, singing a perfectly harmonious song. I found comfort in it and stood there in awe. Suddenly Bret appeared beside me—I hadn't heard him coming. He asked me if everything was okay.

"Hear that? Isn't it the most peaceful sound ever?" I said.

"Jules, wait 'til you see this place. It's so beautiful. I can't wait to show you everything."

Bret was really trying to pull me out of my funk. I felt bad for him and told him I'd try to be myself on this trip. I knew in my heart that he loved me, but just didn't know what to do with me.

We checked into the beautiful bed and breakfast. I wished I felt as crisp and clean as the house was. Everything was a brilliant white with splashes of light green. The bedding was luxurious and filled with fluffy goose down. The house was furnished with antiques and had creaky hardwood floors. Our private bathroom was filled with herbal soaps and hand creams that smelled like rosemary and lavender. I took in the scents, knowing I wouldn't be able to find such things back in Calgary.

I lay on the plump, crisp bed and waited for Bret to finish his shower so I could have a bath in the old claw-foot bathtub. There was a light knock on the door and a voice inviting us down for sandwiches and tea.

We spent that night sitting with the lady of the house, quizzing her about South Africa. Bret, of course, already knew most of the history and could talk to her about it, while I could only listen. I was so proud of him sometimes. Because he was a wrestler, people usually assumed he wasn't very cultured. But Bret was well read and capable of discussing anything with anybody. The hostess was also fascinated with Bret's life. She had never met a wrestler or an actor. Feeling a little left out, I brought up the library and said I wanted to see the Shakespeare folio. She had no clue what I was talking about, and neither did Bret.

Excitedly, I explained that it wasn't an original copy of the plays, but rather a facsimile of what they would have looked like. I heard Bret mutter under his breath that it was a waste of time, and she seemed to agree without saying so. The charm of the Hitman had taken hold. In that instant, I once again felt slighted by his lack of interest in anything I liked or was fascinated by. I stood up and said I was going to bed. Bret started to stand up too, but I was already too hurt, and I think he knew by the look on my face to stay put until I calmed down.

Bret had the next day off, and I woke up hoping he would come with me to the library as a way of making amends for embarrassing me in front of the hostess. I was about to get in the shower when I turned around and blurted out, "Will you come with me?"

"Nah, you go, it's your thing. I'm going to hang out here and go over my script."

I shut the bathroom door quietly, leaned against it and started crying. I don't know why it meant so much to me to have him tag along, but his refusal stirred up all of my old abandonment issues.

I called a cab and waited outside. I didn't even say goodbye. Bret and I shut each other out in silence and went about our business, as we always did. Once in the cab, I asked the driver to stop off at a convenience store. I wanted cigarettes. It was my little way of telling Bret, "Fuck you, I'm sucking on a smoke and you don't even know my dirty little secret." I was pushing him further away, and in an odd way, it empowered me.

When we got to the library I realized that in my haste, I had forgotten to write down our address. I started to panic and asked the driver if he could come back later and take me back to where he'd picked me up. He said sure and handed me his card so I could call him when I was ready. I told myself not to be so empty headed next time.

I entered the library and ran up the stairs as though I was about to greet my secret lover. I couldn't wait to hold the folio in my hands. I rushed to the information desk and asked where it was. The lady at the desk informed me it wasn't just any old book; it was kept in a secured area. I gave her my passport and signed a form saying I wouldn't take any pictures or film it in any way. I had to leave my purse with her and wash my hands before I could see it. A security guard led me to a quiet room, handed me a pair of white gloves, and told me to have a seat. He brought over the largest book I had ever seen. He laid it down in front of me and showed me how to properly turn the pages. I couldn't believe it! I carefully turned each page in wonderment, imagining that I was witnessing the writing of the greatest literature of all time. Time stood still. I sat there and read and read and read.

I went back to the house energized and uplifted. I ran upstairs to tell Bret about my great day, only to rush into an empty room. He left a note saying he had gone out with a promoter to do some radio stuff and would be back soon. I fell back onto the bed with a smile on my face, knowing I had seen basically the coolest book ever.

When Bret returned, he instantly noticed the change in my mood. I told him about my day, and he seemed genuinely interested, for a change. "I'm glad you're so excited, like a little kid, Crabby. The simple things move you sometimes." For the first time in a long time I had a renewed hope for us.

The next day Bret surprised me with a drive up the coast in an Aston Martin he'd borrowed from a friend. He wanted to show me Chapman's Peak, a tourist site famous for its beautiful sunsets. Bret was definitely a romantic, I'll give him that. He always tried so hard to make things perfect for us, though I sometimes suspected he was more interested in control than romance.

We passed through Cape Town to reach the coast. It was such an incredible drive: The long winding highway with its scary cliffs, and the beautiful waves crashing below us reminded me of our relationship. I wanted to make sense of what was going on in my heart, but I couldn't.

When we got there, we parked the car and walked to the lookout point. It was crowded with other people, so Bret and I went and found our own private viewing spot. He was really trying to "show me the world," as he put it once, but at the time the world was too dark for me.

He held my hand and said, "Someday we'll come back here together. When I'm retired I promise to watch the sun go down with you always." I suddenly felt sorry for all the times I'd been unkind to him. I loved him and knew he was making an effort, but I didn't expect it to last.

As the sun began its slow dip into the ocean, I put my head on Bret's chest and silently begged him to never leave me. I vowed to straighten myself out and fix my broken mind. I wanted to purge every toxic thought I had running through my head so I could become a better wife and a better person. That scene lasted only a few moments before I ruined it by starting to videotape the sunset, much to Bret's annoyance. I always felt compelled to record such moments so I could share them with others. It drove Bret nuts.

The next day we went on safari at Kruger Park. I had imagined wild acres of roaming animals, and was surprised when we arrived to thirty-foot-tall fences and lions that looked like they were expecting our arrival. Once you got past the fences, everything was beautiful. Inside the park, there was a gorgeous lodge and swimming pool. The private accommodations were straw huts, which worried me. The staff assured me that they were safe, though I was later told to be careful around the pool at night because a leopard had been seen lurking about. I needed a smoke. I asked a bellboy if there was anywhere I could buy smokes, and he started to laugh. He said I'd have to drive forty miles to a village to buy them.

"My husband doesn't know I smoke. Does someone here smoke? I would pay them American money."

"One of the cleaners does, but I don't know if they are American leaves."

"Oh, okay, but I don't want that kind." I thought he meant pot, though he was actually just talking about the kind of tobacco. He gave me a confused look, but promised to get me cigarettes by the end of the night.

Bret and I were lounging in the lodge when I saw my little bellboy friend again. He was giving me the eye, letting me know that he'd gotten the smokes. I told Bret I'd forgotten something in the room and would be right back. He was too busy chatting with the bartender about ice wine to suspect anything. I snuck off towards my room with the bellboy in tow. He handed me five rollies, and I gave him a twenty for his trouble. I quietly asked him if they would make me go loco. He laughed again, "It's okay leaves."

I went into the bathroom and lit one up. Not bad, I thought—sure tastes like a Marlboro. After I finished I felt faint. It must have been the withdrawal. I went back to the bar and joined Bret for our first night under the stars.

In the morning we headed out on safari. We got into a big, open Hummer and were greeted by a man with a shotgun. I asked him if he'd ever had to use it. He said he had, but hoped he wouldn't need to today. A voice came over the radio, giving our driver directions to where animals were feeding. We slowly drove over to some bushes, where a lioness was feeding on a gazelle it had just caught. We continued to drive and were coming out of a clearing when suddenly our driver stopped and said, "Don't say anything. Shhh. I am going to back up slowly and hopefully it won't charge. It could turn this whole truck over." In front of us stood a huge rhino, looking like Jim Neidhart, Bret's enormous old tag-team partner. I clung to Bret as it stomped its feet to scare us off. It looked like it wanted to charge right at us. I was thinking to myself, of all the fucking ways to die—here's a big Jim Neidhart about to charge at us and trample us to death!

Our driver slowly backed up and the rhino walked off. It was incredible. We headed back to have dinner under the stars. Bret put his arm around me and we both looked up at the most brilliant stars I had ever seen. In the clear sky, they looked like they were twinkling and dancing only a few feet above us. Bret said they were so bright because there was so little pollution in South Africa. He kissed my forehead and said, "Julie, I'd do the stars with you anytime." I never wanted the moment to end. This was what I'd always wanted with him. This was Bret and Julie.

We had to fly to Johannesburg to meet up with Vince McMahon. We got a room at the opulent Michelangelo hotel, which was like a palace, full of marble floors and gold chandeliers. Bret had to leave to do more promotional work, and I was left in the room to brood. I felt the romance of the previous night slipping away as Bret returned to his normal routine. I turned on the television and burst into tears when I saw a family strolling hand-in-hand on a beach in a commercial. I cried deeply until I embarrassed myself back into the present. I wondered what the fuck was wrong with me. The next thing I knew, I was in the minibar fridge, pounding back whatever little bottle found its way into my hands. I was sabotaging everything again.

At breakfast, I was reading the paper when a story caught my eye. I mentioned it to Bret and asked him what he thought about it, but he didn't respond. Apparently something had caught his eye as well. I repeated my question, but he just continued to rubberneck at something in the distance, completely oblivious. I leaned over to see what he was looking at, and there, several yards away, was a topless sunbather. I could see she had quite the rack, even from that distance. I nudged him with my foot and asked him what was so interesting. He didn't answer and just kept staring at the girl. Finally, I stood up, threw the paper at him, and told him to be a little more respectful around me. A blank stare was his only reply. I flew off to our room and slammed the door. He followed me up and started yelling at me for always ruining trips. He said this was the last time he would ever take me overseas. I got up and started to throw things into my suitcase. He asked what I was doing, and I told him to fuck off. He pushed me onto the bed, and I let him have it with a barrage of insults. He lifted me off the bed by my hair and slammed me onto the floor. I was so shocked that I just sat there and started to cry. "I want to go home. Right fucking now Bret. I want to leave. I don't want to be in the same room as you. If you don't send me home, I will find someone who will. Just fucking do it!"

He grabbed my suitcase and threw it against the door. "Get the fuck out, I've had it with you. We are fucking done. I will put you on a plane tonight, but don't ever expect to win me back." With those words, we left for the airport. As Bret stood at the counter arranging my flight, I looked past him out the window—the sun had indeed gone down.

Part One:
The Wild Years
(1970s)

At thirteen years old I was already a veteran runaway. I'd spent countless nights on the street, sleeping in abandoned cars, or hidden in my friends' bedrooms. I was aware of the danger and was often scared shitless by nightfall, but all I really cared about was escaping my stepmom, Mary. I could only run for so long before I was caught. Usually I was brought home, but on one occasion I was sent to Dale's House, a detention centre for runaways.

As soon as I arrived at that dreadful place, I was subjected to one of the most humiliating experiences of my life. I was told to strip down and spread my legs while the custodian poured Kwellada on top of my head to delouse me. I stood there with the Kwellada burning my eyes, my arms tucked in tightly, trying to hide my young, budding body.

How anyone could shame and violate a thirteen-year-old girl in such a way is beyond me. It is such an awkward and vulnerable age to begin with, let alone with someone standing over you, telling you to spread your legs without explaining why. To this day I'm uncomfortable without clothing on, even when sleeping. After my delousing I was taken to a room I would share with another girl, and given flannel pajamas to sleep in. The custodian told me the rules of conduct and informed me about the routines of the detention centre. I was to get up and make my bed and be in the breakfast hall before 7:00 a.m. If I was tardy I wouldn't be allowed to eat until lunch. I lay in the stiff, small cot and cried when she shut the door.

There was little comfort in that room, except for the softness of my pajamas, which reminded me of a cozy summer I had spent at my grandma's house. The faint glimmer of the moon shined through the matted window guards, reminding me I wouldn't be escaping anytime soon. There was no hope of going anywhere.

The next day, I awoke to the sight of my roommate sitting on her bed with her hands folded carefully on her lap. She stared at me and didn't say a word. As we made our beds she turned on her 45 record player and played "Cathy's Clown," by The Everly Brothers. In the coming weeks it would be all she ever played.

Filing into the breakfast hall, not a word was exchanged between any of us. Looking back, it reminds me of the scene in *One Flew Over the Cuckoo's Nest* where they line up to get their medication one by one. Those who were accustomed to the routine shuffled and swayed slowly to their designated areas. Gravitating towards the taller kids, as I did when I wanted to seem older, I pulled a chair back to sit down and was quickly told to "move it" by one of the Native girls. Although this was the area I was supposed to be in, this was not the chair I was to sit in. Keeping my head down, I moved to the next chair and was again told to "move it." I eventually ended up at the very end of the table. I didn't mind because it meant not talking to anyone. Breakfast was as I had imagined it would be: oatmeal, with unbuttered toast and orange juice. The younger kids were the only ones who spoke freely or emitted any sort of laughter. The girls at the other end of my table spoke in low voices and shared their thoughts amongst themselves. I eventually picked up on their common dialect and slang, which was mostly new to me. I had no idea yet that I too was of Aboriginal descent. I had gone to school with Native kids, but nobody had ever called me a "half-breed" or a "nitchy." It wasn't until I went to live with Mom that I found out I was a "half-breed."

I passed the time just watching TV and walking around alone outside, hoping to be released from this small prison. The girls weren't friendly, especially to newcomers. The girl I roomed with slept on her bed most of the day, when not attending the makeshift school they had set up in a separate building. She seemed despondent, and I would often find her in the fetal position listening to that "Cathy's Clown" record over and over. I wondered why such a young girl was so fixated on a song that seemed to be about a man leaving a woman for someone else. In retrospect, it must have been a father figure in her young life that she thought of while that record spun around and around.

Every day I waited for some news about what I was doing here. Was I staying? Or, worse yet, was I going to be sent somewhere else? I asked if Mom had called at all, or Dad. I always got a curt no. I was relieved that Dad hadn't called, because at least that meant I wasn't going back to his house. I vividly recalled the constant sparring with Mary that had led me here and knew that as I got older and better at fighting back, I would become less controllable and more threatening to her. My mind flashed back to the latest incident; my face broke into a smug smile as I recalled grappling with her and squeezing her boob as hard as I could. She had yelped in pain and shock at my sudden action, and had flown out of the room yelling that I was out of there forever. It was a turning point in our relationship: it showed her that I was going to give it out as good as I was getting it. My days as her whipping post were over, though she certainly had Dad whipped enough to keep me out of the house.

One day while watching TV a few of the older girls nudged the back of the couch and asked if I smoked. I didn't, but, wanting to appear cool to them, I gave a lazy "yeah." Of course, none of us had access to cigarettes as we were all underage, but one of the girls had stolen some from a counsellor's purse. I was asked to "keep six" while they smoked, and in return I was accepted into their gang. I shrugged like I was unaffected by their sudden interest in me. I had to remain cool or I would be relegated to that lonely chair at the end of the table every morning.

When they finished smoking and came back into the common room, they started asking me questions about why I was there. I told them I was a chronic runaway, and that I just wanted to go back to living with my mom. Many of them were trying to get away from their parents or parent, agreeing that life on the street was better than life with their families. They started talking about drinking and fighting, and a couple of them admitted to sex with older boys. I was in awe of their stories and started to see that there was a whole other world out there, apart from the one I knew. My only contribution to the conversation was telling them how I evaded the cops. Unimpressed, they started laughing and saying that anyone could hide from the pigs. I didn't even know what they meant by "pigs"—it wasn't anything I had heard before.

The next day we were all questioned separately about who had stolen the cigarettes. I had been made aware of the code of the street and didn't say a word when it was my turn, knowing there would be trouble if I talked. I just claimed that those girls never talked to me, and so I had no way of knowing about the cigarettes. We were all confined to our rooms, with no privileges, for two days. I preferred lying in my bed to finding out what the girls did to "rats." I lay there, daydreaming about being a part of their gang.

I was asked to come to the office, because my social worker was there to see me. I was surprisingly happy to talk to her, despite my growing realization that all of the adults in the facility were fucked and didn't give a shit about you. The gang told me that the social workers, and their promises to help, were just part of the bigger lie. I put their words aside and excitedly asked about my mom, and whether she knew I was here, and when I could leave. The social worker said that there hadn't been a court order yet, and that as far as she knew they were only talking to my dad and stepmother, who were quite adamant about me not returning back there. Mary had claimed I was a disruption to my siblings. I continued to press the social worker about my mother. "Does my mom know I'm here?" Again she responded with the court order situation and that was it. I dug my nails into my hands and wanted to rip the flesh out of my palms, I was so frustrated. I asked if I could call my mom and tell her myself that I wanted to live with her. She assured me that that wasn't going to happen; my dad had full custody now, so it was up to him.

I became like my roommate and stayed in the fetal position until the next morning, when I was awoken by a counsellor who told me I would be starting school that day, and needed to go to the office to pick up some supplies for my classes. I was never a good student as I daydreamed a lot, and escaped by reading anything I could get my hands on—especially stories that promised a happy ending.

By now my vocabulary mainly consisted of the f-word and a few choice epithets inspired by female anatomy. The women who worked at the detention centre were the only ones I referred to as "cunts." It was my new favourite word and I reserved it for all the loathsome counsellors and custodians who roamed the facility. To show off my new rebellious attitude and get a laugh from the other kids, I would flip off the teachers (or anyone else, for that matter). Another trick I had was to contort my face and mimic the teachers as they wrote on the blackboards. I lacked respect for myself and others, and I would carry this attitude with me for many years.

The next few weeks were filled with misbehaviour and escapism in the glorified stories of my new friends. I found myself speaking and acting like them, picking on the weaker kids, though not the younger ones as some did. Most of the time it was about their weight or some idiotic quirk they had. Oddly, no one ever bothered the Cathy's Clown girl; we all left her to her own misery. Everyone seemed guarded in their own way, and as I walked down the hallways I imagined what their lives were like outside of these walls. I suspected most of them had been sexually abused by who knows who, because they all had such a dislike for men or anyone in an authoritative position. Today, knowing the signs of sexual abuse, I'd be willing to bet that they had all been through something terrible.

I was sitting around watching soaps with everyone when I was called to the office. My social worker was sitting with one of the counsellors when I walked in, and they told me to have a seat.

The counsellor then nonchalantly told me I'd be leaving in a few days. "The courts have agreed to give your mom custody." I had never felt so thrilled. I asked, "When exactly will I be leaving?" They said as soon as they received the paperwork I'd be on my way home. I jumped out of my chair and went to share the news, but I didn't exactly get the kind of reception I was hoping for. The kids seemed pissed off at me, and tried to downplay my excitement by saying I would be back in here before I knew it. I felt anxious and rejected at the time, but looking back I realize it was their way of expressing that they wished they could go home to someone too.

Mom tried to make the transition as easy as possible for me, and I was delighted to be with my older sister Sandy, who was fifteen. The only problem was our stepdad, Herb—a man I loathed for taking our mother away those many years ago. He was 6'4" and towered over me, eyeing me with suspicion from day one. He had icy blue eyes, just like Mary's, an abnormally big nose, and gigantic ears which became the focus of my teasing whenever I felt like pissing him off. We didn't talk to each other much in the beginning, which suited me fine as I couldn't bear to look at him without wondering what Mom saw in him. My dislike for him eventually spilled over to the children he had with Mom. I was very cold to them and resented them for what had happened between my own parents. Sad really, when I think back and see the immaturity of my behaviour.

Herb made it frightfully clear, right from the beginning, that I was not welcome. When Mom wasn't around he wouldn't feed me or allow me to eat any of the food he purchased. He only bought enough groceries to feed himself and the other children. Mom was working and had no idea what he was doing. His idea of a meal for his kids was frozen fries and a can of meatballs and gravy. Sometimes he would switch it up and give them canned ravioli. The only time there was real food was when Mom went shopping after getting paid. Otherwise we were left to fend for ourselves.

Sandy and I would lie in bed at night with her little plastic radio, waiting for our favourite songs to come on. We had a ritual of not going to sleep until we heard "Angie" by The Rolling Stones or "Baby Blue" by Badfinger. Sometimes Herb would pound on the floor, threatening to switch off the power if we didn't "shut that pig music off." He would often go down to the basement and actually flip the switch. That's how hateful he would get at the slightest provocation. In turn, so would I. I would mockingly grunt and snort like a pig as he made his way back upstairs. Sandy would laugh her ass off, covering her head with a blanket to avoid pissing him off further.

For the most part, there wasn't any physical abuse. However, there was one incident where things got violent between Herb and me. Sandy and I came home from school a little early one day and didn't expect Herb to be home. He had locked the front door, even though he was well aware that we'd be coming home from school. So, feeling agitated, I kicked the door a little too hard. Then I pounded on the glass part of the door just as loudly. Sandy warned me not to be so loud. "He's gonna freak on you," she whispered. It would have irritated the shit out of me, too, if someone had been carrying on that way.

The door suddenly flew open and Herb gave chase like a greyhound after a rabbit. I laughed hysterically as he chased me, probably out of surprise at his sudden appearance. I slipped on the grass and he swooped over top of me with a wet cloth and started hitting me with it. I kicked back, yelling at him to fuck off and leave me alone. His face went beet red as he called me a "Smadu Bastard" and berated me for "trying to wreck his stuff." Mom walked around the corner with two bags of groceries, which she dropped when she saw what was happening. She came running over and punched him in the back, saying shrilly, "Don't you ever hit my kids again. Fuck off and leave her alone."

To me it was a major victory, as it showed my mother how abusive he was and gave me quiet hope that she would leave him.

My teasing escalated from that point on. We glared at each other like alley cats in the following months, and I did everything I could to further agitate him. I mocked and imitated him relentlessly. When Herb and Mom sat on the couch, I would sit beside her and mimic his every move. Mom would have to yell, "Stop that, you crazy kid!" because sometimes I would jokingly try to put my hand in her shirt like he did. I thought he was a pig for doing it and never really considered that it might have been their way of being affectionate. But Christ, did he have to do it front of everyone?

I could tell their relationship was slowly disintegrating. The signs were subtle at first: Mom started spending some nights with the kids in their bedroom, for instance. It wasn't until she started drinking again and disappearing with her sisters that their problems became undeniable. Herb cursed Mom's family as a bunch of pimps and whores from the northern, poorer end of town.

Luckily I had a mix of friends from different backgrounds to distract me from my home life. At school there were nice, well-mannered, Catholic white kids from middle-class families. My other friends were badass Native girls. Many of them came from unstable homes, something I could relate to. There wasn't that sense of being in a gang, as there had been at the detention centre, but a sense of belonging because our lives were so alike. It was nice to be able to go back and forth between groups of friends, but I preferred the ones who lived on the edge and had little parental supervision, because it meant we could get away with things like skipping school. Most of the time we hung out at their houses, because their parents were usually too hungover to even notice us.

Nobody seemed to give a shit until the school sent a truant officer named Mrs. Woods after us. Mrs. Woods had unbelievably vile breath and bright, painted red lips. I pulled my t-shirt up over my mouth and nose and slouched in my chair while she gave me an excruciatingly long speech about skipping school. When she brought my mother in to speak with her, I foolishly argued that

I should be able to stay home from school and babysit, just like my sister, Sandy. Her eyes narrowed behind her stupid cat-eye glasses as she peered at me and questioned me. Mom looked embarrassed, as though a horrible secret had been told. Sandy hadn't missed as many days as I had, but she was nonetheless missing school, and that was a serious offence in the Catholic school system. I knew I would be in trouble for letting that slip, because it really incriminated Mom, who had been writing Sandy notes for her absences with phony excuses. Pissed off, Mom gave her an "Ah, fuck, it's none of your business what I do." She offered her help and assured Mom a lot could be done. Before she left, Mom made a point of telling Mrs. Woods her lipstick was too red and her breath stank to high hell. That was the end of Mrs. Woods.

Angie became my best friend in grade seven. I loved hanging out with her because she was a quiet, easy-going kid who knew plenty of cool people outside of school. I stayed at her house on the weekends and wouldn't come home until Sunday night. Her mom, who was Aboriginal, and her dad, who was German, didn't seem to mind me being there all the time and probably felt relieved that Angie had someone to hang out with while they drank all night. Sometimes we would head over to Angie's grandma's house, where I usually elected to watch the drinking fests with curiosity, rather than indulge in them. God knows the booze flowed freely—and when there wasn't alcohol, they drank vanilla extract. Angie's grandmother smelled like a cookie factory. She was a tiny little Native woman with no teeth, but she had the sweetest disposition. She would often ask me to go and get more vanilla from the store, knowing it would be easier for me because I looked white. As long as there was booze or vanilla everyone remained happy. If they ran out, everyone would just go to bed and shut down until the next day. They were the only family out of everyone I knew who never fought.

Occasionally I'd break from those friends and hang out with my jock friend, Maggie. She was the prettiest girl I'd ever seen, with a Dove-girl complexion and perfect teeth. If there is such a thing as an all–Canadian girl, she was the perfect image of it. The only problem was her parents. They were overbearing Hungarian immigrants with a "spare the rod, spoil the child" mentality. They were always beating Maggie for something, and it only made her rebel further. We would sneak out on weekends and go joyriding with our older friends Glen and Rick. Glen would take us out to the country to show us his supposed driving skills while fishtailing and swigging beer. Maggie, tomboy that she was, gleefully threw empties at road signs with better aim than any of the boys. We would stay out until the sun was ready to crest in the early morning, and then race to get Maggie home before her parents noticed she was gone. Sometimes she would get caught just as she was easing herself in through her window, and we'd know it would be a few weeks until she'd be able to sneak out again.

At home, I began to feel sorry for Herb. He looked so forlorn whenever Mom would take off with her sisters, and would pitifully ask me to help track her down. I would sit in the car while he peered through the windows of hotel lounges looking for her. He was a horribly jealous man, always checking Mom's neck to see if another man had left some telltale sign of passion. Whenever she slept in the kids' room, he would creep in with a flashlight to check on her. Mom would sometimes ask to sleep with me, knowing full well he wouldn't bother her if I was in the room. These were their fighting tactics; they would hold out on each other. She would refuse to sleep in his bed, he would refuse to buy food for the family.

It was sad to see the kids caught in the middle, and it was even sadder when Christmas rolled around and Herb refused to buy anything. No tree, no presents, and worst of all, no food. Mom complained to her mom about it, and before we knew it my 5'2" grandmother showed up like a raging twister. She marched right into the house, trailed by my uncle Don, and started hitting Herb with a broom. It must have felt degrading to him, to have his kids and everyone else watch him get beaten up by a little old lady. She berated him with a flurry of expletives until my uncle stepped in, physically picking her up and moving her. That gave Herb a chance to run to the bathroom and lock himself in, though it didn't stop her from yelling through the door that he was a big-nosed German bastard who was mistreating her grandkids. He regained enough courage to yell at her to go back to the north end of town, where she belonged. Not too long after that, Mom moved us out. She was finished with his jealousy and the way he deprived the kids of so much.

Whoever said we live in a white man's world obviously hadn't been to Regina. For the next few years all I knew was how to survive the red way. My friends at the time would take me very deeply into this world. It all began one night when a group of us decided to go to a house party.

We showed up at a tiny little house a few blocks from mine, and I had my first look at true ghetto living. Some of the windows were broken and the furniture looked like it had been dragged in from a junkyard. The floors felt crispy under our feet and I don't even think the heat was on—you could see your breath when you talked. The beer bottles gently stuck to your lips when you took too long a sip, so you had to guzzle quickly. We all huddled around and tapped our feet and drank to keep warm. Some of the people there were sniffing glue. Every once and while they would take out a new tube and refill the bag, gently coaxing the glue to stay soft by moving it in circular motions.

I turned to someone and asked what they were doing. "Sniffing," the person answered nonchalantly. Not wanting to appear stupid, I didn't enquire further. An older girl came over to us, and my friend Maria introduced me as "Hunt," which was my nickname. I started to explain the name, but the older girl seemed unimpressed and looked past me as I spoke. I felt embarrassed and was starting to wish I were elsewhere when she unexpectedly asked me for my full name.

"Julie Smadu," I said.

"You're Sandy's sister?"

"Yeah."

"Your sis is cool. I go to school with her. She's the only white broad in that school that's nice to me." I quickly corrected that we were actually half-Indian. She started laughing and said, "You don't look Indian to me. Who's the Indian?"

"My mom. My grandmother's Eva Lapierre."

"Are you shitting me? Do you have an uncle named Ken?"

"Yeah, he's Mom's brother."

"What I wouldn't do to chippy him at least once."

Suddenly the party crowd seemed to part and this tall boy appeared, looking like Brad Pitt coming over the horizon in Legends of the Fall. I just stared at him, with his full lips and flowing brown hair, like I had never seen a human before. He walked up to the girl I had been talking to, kissed her, and led her to the tiny freezing cold bedroom down the hall.

I was exploring my youth at a furious pace, which meant not being home, or at school. There was one girl in particular, whose name I won't mention, who became a terrible influence on me. I found myself falling deep into her world, which consisted of drugs, booze, and making money, though she did her best to protect me from the worst of it. Young as she was, she had already committed armed robbery a few times and collected a variety of aliases. I was never involved in anything like that, but I saw enough of it to develop some street smarts and learn how to stay out of trouble, even when it was all around me.

For a while my closest cohorts were Maria and Lisa. We'd spend our days experimenting with acid, among other things. We would each take a hit and then just wander through town, sometimes stopping by the Woolco to look around and eat chocolate, amazed at how it melted between our fingers. We'd giggle until we got kicked out and told never to return again. On more than one morning I woke up and took another hit, starting the whole thing all over again. Or I'd wake up outside, under the bridge in Wascana, where we'd sometimes sleep.

I hadn't started dating yet, but I did have a plenty of crushes, especially on older guys like Ron and Roger, who were friends of Sandy's boyfriend. They both seemed to like me, so I had to drop not-so-subtle hints about who I was more interested in, like rhyming our names together: Julie Smadu and Roger Goodu forever. I also had a thing for Calvin, a tall, handsome Indian boy, who was friends with my cousin Luke. I would hang out with them and their friends Darryl, Darcy, and Dwayne, also known as Bummer. I remember Bummer coming to my door with a handful of jewelry—he had stolen it from someone's home and remembered that I always wore a couple of chains. I accepted them, but never really stole myself; my thievery was limited to raiding gardens for vegetables and my sister's closet for clothes.

There was one incident where I ended up behind the wheel of a stolen car. Luke had stolen a car from the dealership across the street from my dad's house and wanted to go for a joyride. He picked us all up and we drove all the way to Lestock before turning around. I had to drive back because everyone else was too high on speed. We never got caught, and we never tried it again.

Out of all my cousins, I had the most fun with Luke, though we tended to be a bad influence on each other. We tried sniffing for the first time that winter. We were in an alley behind Mom's house, where cars were always parked. Luke took the cap off some guy's tank and we got really high, laughing and giggling so loudly that the car's owner came out to see what was going on. "You fucking Indians! Get away from my car!" he screeched. We could barely run, we were so stoned from the fumes. I remember telling Luke I couldn't feel my tongue—it felt like rubber in my mouth. Talk about massive headaches. Sniffing puts an expensive wine hangover to shame. We later found out from other kids that you could sniff Ban underarm deodorant if you sprayed it onto a Kleenex first. We tried that at my aunt's house, when we babysat for her. I wonder if she ever figured out why her cans were always empty. This little phase didn't last long because the headaches where unbearable, and we were more into acid.

Once again, I found myself doing whatever I could to avoid the difficult situation at home. After leaving Herb, Mom moved all of us into an unbearably crowded townhouse. There wasn't nearly enough room for Mom, the kids, a now-pregnant Sandy, her boyfriend Wayne, and me. I often found myself sleeping on the floor in front of the stereo. As if that wasn't enough, Mom was always playing host to our partying relatives, who proved to be a serious burden.

Uncle Howard and Uncle Dick would come over with friends and whatever flavour-of-the-month girlfriends they had and eat and drink themselves silly. These somewhat joyful occasions usually ended in pathetic arguments, with Mom venting her frustrations over her life's disappointments. All of her repressed emotions would come gurgling up after a few rum and Cokes, and she would pick a fight with anyone she thought was disagreeing with her in the slightest. Uncle Howard, with his genial manner and baby blue Hank Williams suit tucked into cowboy boots, was always the one to try and calm her down, but more often than not the best thing to do was just to get up and leave.

These meltdowns were more frequent around Christmas, after Mom endured the annual humiliation of asking for handouts like the Christmas hamper offered by the Salvation Army. I helped where I could, buying a tree and presents for the kids. It angered me to see her squandering what little we had on everyone who passed through the house; all the guests meant there would be no leftovers for the days to come, in a house that often had nothing in the fridge except a jar of beets, Crisco, and a small quart of milk. We would fight and I would take off again, leaving her to her drinking. I now see that, on some level, she wanted to share with others even when she had nothing, and wish I had been a little more understanding of her struggles.

Those years were hard for Mom, and her drinking escalated when she felt ashamed. Though she was rid of Herb, she soon met a new man named Bill, who was the biggest leech of them all. He only came around when he was drunk, and was uninterested in any real intimacy. Everyone pushed her to get rid of him and told her that he was just using her. She ignored them, but I'm sure she admitted the truth to herself when she was alone at night with her thoughts. I remember waking up many times to the sound of him throwing up violently, and wondering why she put up with someone so beneath her. I would, of course, wonder the same thing about myself and Bret, thirty years later, in the murky moments of our post-divorce affairs.

I was about to turn sixteen when Dad showed up at Mom's to ask me if I would help him take care of my siblings Mark and Michelle. I thought maybe he was trying to get back together with Mom, but I knew it wouldn't happen—she wasn't that desperate. He said he needed help because he was worried social services would take them away. It turned out he and Mary were having marital problems, and that she had been taking off for long periods of time. He mentioned that she had met someone else. I felt like cheering, but replied, "Whatever, Dad, just let me know when you need help."

I met up with my friend Cindy and asked her if she would come check out the situation at Dad's with me. I was worried Mary would return, and wanted someone there to watch my back in case things got out of hand. When we arrived the kids were very happy to see me. I was surprised by Michelle's height as she stood beside her brother; I couldn't remember the last time I'd seen them. I asked them where Dad was, and they said he had gone out to look for Mary. My stepsiblings Charlene and

Philip were there too, but regrettably, I resented them too much to be nice to them, and made them stay in their rooms while the rest of us hung out and played records. Michelle was listening to the Bay City Rollers at the time and it made me realize how innocent their lives were. Mark had a paper route that Michelle would help him with, even if she had to be bullied into doing so. At the end of the night Dad came home and went straight to bed; I suppose he was embarrassed that he had been out looking for Mary. Cindy and I stuck around and made breakfast for the kids in the morning before Dad left again to go to work, or to look for Mary. That night Cindy and I drank beer, turned up the music and danced around with Michelle, while Mark sat quietly watching TV. I suppose he didn't quite know what to make of me or the situation. Perhaps, in his young mind, he didn't see Mary leaving as a positive thing, or perhaps he didn't believe it would be permanent. I had waited a long time for this to happen and I was probably the most elated that Dad had escaped his terrible fate, though he would soon manage to recreate it with Gloria.

Mary would make a final return, showing up on a Saturday evening in all her semi-naked glory, with Dad trailing behind her. I remember the drunken, confused look on her face when she stumbled in and saw me.

"What the fuck are you doing here?" she demanded.

"You fucking whore, you haven't changed!" was my reply, coming from years of anger and hatred.

She then screeched for my dad to get me out of the house. I stood my ground, but Dad, probably relieved to have her home, asked me to leave. As we continued to fight and scream at each other, Michelle ran to her room and Mark took off outside. Mary tried to punch Dad, but fell down and missed, which made me burst out into laughter and taunts. Dad again said he thought I should leave. I told him he was as fucked as she was and headed out the door with Cindy.

I met up with Lisa again and continued partying, never expecting the fun to suddenly turn to terror. Lisa and I were hitchhiking on Albert Street when we were picked up by our attacker. He was young and didn't appear menacing or dangerous. We asked for a ride to south Albert Street, but when we got there he kept going. He told us not to worry, that he just wanted to have a few beers with us, but ended up taking us out of town on a dirt road. I wasn't sixteen yet, but I had enough street sense to know this was going to be trouble. I started talking tough and swore a lot, as if that would scare him off. He asked how old I was, and I said I was sixteen, though looking back it was probably the wrong thing to tell him; things may have gone differently if he had known I was only fifteen and Lisa was only fourteen. He seemed to be more interested in Lisa, but, without going into details about it, I was the one he decided to rape. I hate to imagine how much worse it could have gone if we hadn't made our escape, which was like something out of a movie. I told him we had to go to the bathroom, and after he reluctantly agreed, we hopped out of the car and I told Lisa to fucking run and not stop. There was a forest beside the road and we ran deep into the trees in case he decided to get out of his car and come after us. I remember lying in the snow, watching him drive back and forth for what seemed like hours, yelling out the window, "I will fucking kill you bitches when I find you!" He eventually gave up and drove off.

Thank God it wasn't that cold of a night because we were still a long way from home. As we walked we saw a farmer driving home and waved him down. He pulled over and let us in the truck, and we both talked so frantically about what had happened that he couldn't understand what was going on. Eventually we managed to spit it out and asked to be driven to the police station. He drove us to Mom's instead, perhaps not wanting to get involved. We got to Mom's and then, stupidly, hitchhiked to the police station.

I tried to move on and resume a normal life. I moved back in with Dad and my siblings, not realizing I was pregnant. I asked Lisa something that I had been curious about for a while. I asked her why I hadn't gotten my period, and she looked shocked at the question.

"Since when?" she asked.

"This month it didn't come," I said.

"Fuck, you're probably pregnant."

I had never even considered that because no one had ever talked to me about birth control or sex, and it honestly seemed like the least obvious answer at the time. "I noticed my pants getting a little tighter lately. How do I find out?" I asked. She told me to go to the doctor's and get a test done.

After she left I sat in a daze, trying to figure out what to do. I knew I didn't want the child of the guy who raped me. My head swirled with fear and shame, and I couldn't make sense of any of it, so I just sat there in silence. As always, I ignored reality and put it off.

After a few weeks I finally went to a doctor and found out I was at least three months pregnant. The personal questions regarding the father were unbearable. I couldn't bring myself to say I had been raped, so I just said we weren't together anymore and left it at that. The doctor gave me some vitamins and sent me on my way. On the walk back to Dad's Lisa suggested I tell the rapist, "you know, that guy in the field."

"Now wouldn't that be fucking smart," I snapped at her.

We walked the rest of the way in silence. Lisa stayed at Dad's for a few more days, until her parents called the police looking for her. I was alone again with my thoughts and fears. To make things worse, her parents decided that I was a bad influence on her and wouldn't even let us talk on the phone.

It was a while before I saw her again; I was further along in my pregnancy and as lost as ever. I suddenly had the bright idea for what I now regard as one of my greatest sins. I told Lisa to get on top of the garage.

"What for?" she asked.

"Because you are going to jump on my stomach, and we'll see if it will come out so I can be over this fucking thing."

"Are you nuts? I'm not doing that!"

"Lise, do you want to help me or not?"

Lisa reluctantly got on top of the garage, perhaps seeing the twisted logic in it. She jumped a few times, and each time nothing happened. We gave up after a while and went into the house. I wondered if Dad's neighbours saw any of it and what they must have thought. To this day I regret what I made her do. The whole thing could have ended with far graver consequences, physically and morally.

"Now what?" I asked.

"What about an abortion?"

"Yeah, who do we call?"

We checked the Yellow Pages, but didn't know what to look for. Lisa called her sister and did the old if a friend wanted an abortion, who could she call routine, but in complete sincerity.

"How far along is she?" her sister asked.

"Four months."

"Too late, it has to be three months or less, and you have to go to the States."

I now felt hopeless and terribly hormonal, and was very difficult to deal with at home. I would get annoyed by stupid little things, like how people chewed. One day I snapped and screamed at Dad, "Do you have to chew like that? It sounds like the bones in your temples are cracking!" Poor Dad had no idea why my moods were so up and down. I was so ashamed I wore his shirts, to make sure no one could see the outline of my belly. The only upside was the dramatic increase in bust size, which I boasted about to Lisa. I avoided Mom. I didn't want her asking any questions. I didn't really go out at all—I just stayed home and ate and watched TV. No one really asked why. The kids didn't understand and Dad was too lost in his own world.

I tried to cheer everyone up by suggesting a trip to Katepwa to barbeque and go swimming. We were all excited, even Dad, who was whistling and calling me "Juler" and reminding me to bring mustard for the dogs. Dad used to take us up there all the time; he loved to fish and barbeque, but hadn't done either in years. Dad swam around with Michelle while Mark busied himself trying to stay underwater for as long as he possibly could. I jumped in the water in my extra-large t-shirt and tried to float on my back—not a good move for a pregnant girl trying to hide her condition. Dad called Lisa and me out of the water; it was time to eat. As I got out the water, Lisa suddenly exclaimed, "Holy shit, look at your tits!" I looked down and saw two giant brown circles showing through my t-shirt, which was clinging to my protruding stomach. Lisa ran out of the water to grab me another shirt, explaining to everyone on the way that I was cold. Man, Dad was gullible at times, and thank goodness for that. As we drove back to Regina, I shook my head and wondered how much longer I could keep this up.

October rolled around and Lisa and I found out we had court. We had charged that guy with rape and it was time for the trial. Instead, we left town, and to this day I still have no idea why. Fear overcame us and logic flew out the window. Lisa and I decided to take off to Saskatoon rather than face the guy, who we worried would get off and decide to come after us. We jumped on a bus after stealing enough money from Lisa's parents for the tickets. Lisa's crazy uncle Dan lived in Saskatoon, and there wasn't a doubt in her mind that he would let us stay with him. In complete ignorance of the legal system, we figured we could wait out the trial in Saskatoon and return when it all blew over.

We got to Saskatoon and went to a hotel, which I would coincidentally return to on my first night with Bret in 1979. Lisa's uncle worked at the hotel and we assumed we'd be able to catch him there. We sat in the hotel restaurant and waited for him to show up. We had enough money for a cup of coffee between us, and that was it. After a failed attempt at finding his number in the phone book and four hours of loitering, we stared to worry. I looked out the window and saw a guy take off his tie and glance in at us. I looked away, feeling like he was looking for us. I told Lisa not to talk to him, no matter what; she looked confused and I hushed her as he came in. He walked over to the counter and ordered a coffee while Lisa and I pretended to be having an intense conversation so he wouldn't bother us. After a couple of minutes, he leaned over and asked how we were doing. We ignored him, but he asked again.

"Why?" I asked sarcastically.

"I don't know. It looks like you girls are kind of looking for company."

"Doubt it."

"So what are you doing here then?"

"Why, you a cop writing a book?"

We started to laugh, but he interrupted us, "Why yes, I am. I'm vice and you girls have been sitting here for an awfully long time and we are curious as to why. Are you looking for action?"

"Are you fucking nuts? We're waiting for her uncle to show up, that's all."

He asked us to come outside, but we refused. He reminded us that he was a cop, and I asked him to prove it. He pulled out his badge, led us outside to his unmarked car, and took us to the station. When we got there he split us up and put us in separate little rooms. After an hour or so he came into my room and told me he knew everything.

"Like what?"

"Are you girls missing a date to appear in court?"

In my mind I cursed Lisa for telling him. I kept denying I knew anything, and could tell he was getting frustrated with me.

"You could get in a lot of trouble for involving an underage girl in all of this."

I sat stunned at what he said, and told him it was Lisa's idea to run.

"You are older than her and she is underage."

"Yeah, so? What does that have to do with me? I didn't twist her arm to come here."

"Well, I can't do anything to you because you are of age, but your girlfriend could be put into a detention centre until her parents send for her. And there's this business of the court date in Regina. You were both supposed to go and I want to know why you didn't."

I tried to explain but he cut me off, "I think maybe you both might be lying about what happened and you felt guilty and took off."

I suddenly felt so angry and screamed, "Fuck off! Leave me alone, you fucking pig! Send me home!"

"Oh, we will, after we talk to Lisa's parents and arrange for transportation."

He left me waiting in that room a long while, and finally returned to tell me that I would be leaving, but not Lisa. He wouldn't answer any of my questions or let me speak with her. I was taken to a bus depot and told to check in with the police once I got home. Lisa and I never ended up in court, because we dropped the charges and were almost charged ourselves with mischief. I guess we were too scared, and, in some foolish way, we felt responsible for the whole thing because we had been hitchhiking.

I was standing in Dad's living room when my water broke. I said to Lisa, "Shit, I'm peeing myself!" Lisa just stood there as the water flowed down my legs. I had no idea what was going on. I called Mom and she immediately told me, "Get to the hospital. Your water broke." It was only then that I found out she knew. I guess she must have known for a while, but never said anything to me about it. Lisa and I called a cab and went to the General, on the other side of the city. When we arrived I spoke in low tones and covered my stomach when I sat, still trying to hide the fact that I was a sixteen-year-old having a baby.

Labour was an excruciating experience that no amount of drugs could make better. The next day I went to have a shower and when I came back I saw that one of the nurses had brought the baby in. I rang the buzzer and said "What are you doing? Come get him!" The nurse apologized and said it had been a mistake. I felt compelled to explain myself and wished I could tell her the whole story, but nothing came out of my mouth.

That night Dad showed up with the kids. He stood in the doorway, and when I told him to come in he looked uncomfortable and averted his eyes when he spoke to me.

"Is there anything you need?" he asked.

"No, Dad. I'm not keeping him."

He asked why not, but I couldn't bring myself to tell him. I asked how he knew I was here. Apparently my Aunt Judy, who was a nurse there on a different floor, had seen me and called him. Dad left after a few minutes, but Michelle and Mark stuck around. Michelle said she had known, but Mark said he just thought I was getting fat. Michelle, in all her wonderment, asked all kinds of questions, which I replied to with half-assed answers.

Mom didn't come up to see me, which was actually kind of a relief. I was tired of the shame.

Sandy called to say she would visit and asked what she should bring. I knew Sandy would be the one to understand; she didn't question me and just wanted to help. I told her I would really appreciate it if she brought me a shirt and bought me some new pants.

"What size?"

"Twenty-eight."

"You're not a twenty-eight, you just had a baby."

"I'm sure I'll squeeze into something by tomorrow."

I think on a subconscious level I wanted to believe nothing had happened to me. Denial is a great defence against shame, and I just wanted to get out of there so I could put it all behind me.

In the coming months I would do nothing but drink and fall into a haze of pot to help me forget. I started to feel as though it had happened a lifetime ago. Lisa and I started hanging out with Sandy and her friends, and continued to try and act older than we were. Winter came and went, and I don't remember much of it, probably because of what we had been doing. Dad was still in his own world and did nothing but work and sleep. Michelle and Mark started hanging out with our cousins on Mom's side of the family, which seemed safe to me. In the meantime, I was more in charge of my own life than ever, and had no sense of purpose or direction.

For most people, turning seventeen is an exciting occasion, with adulthood just over the horizon. You wonder what you will do after high school, worry about all the usual teenage things, and wish you were eighteen. That is, of course, if you'd been given enough support and direction from your parents to feel confident about your future. Unfortunately, I hadn't, and I accepted life for what it was at the time. I had already seen a lot and lived a lot by most standards, and it was enough that I just not end up like most of the women I knew. I didn't want to become a junkie or live off welfare with five kids from five different fathers.

Everything seemed to be going smoothly at Dad's until he came home one evening with his new girlfriend, whom he'd met at the Lonely Hearts Club, a seedy singles bar. She didn't make a very good first impression on me. I think what threw me was the wig, obviously stolen from some mannequin with a different head size. Or maybe it was the gown? I jokingly asked if they had just been ballroom dancing. Dad ignored my question and said, "This is Gloria." I refused to shake the hand of someone who looked like an oversized, overweight Barbie doll. I just nodded, went downstairs, and turned up Led Zeppelin as loud as I could.

It wasn't long before she showed up with a suitcase in one hand and a birdcage in the other, ready to move in. It was then that I developed a twitch in my tail. Mark, Michelle, and I would be relentless in our efforts to get rid of her. Gloria made herself at home in no time, rearranging the furniture and filling the air with some noxious disinfectant.

"What the fuck is that smell?" I asked Dad.

Gloria jumped in, "You shouldn't swear around Michelle and Mark. It's not nice."

"Are you fucking kidding me? I was talking to Dad, not you."

So there was one of my weapons; my use of foul language was going to get her.

I realize now that she meant well, but I had so much anger built up before she even came on the scene that it was hard not to project it onto her. She tried to be nice at first, but her patience quickly ran out and soon the battle was on.

We fought constantly for the next few months, picking on each other's weaknesses. My biggest concern was for Mark and Michelle. I was at Mom's when Michelle called. She was extremely upset at Gloria— just that name made me drop the phone and run to Dad's. When I got there Gloria was pretending to be busy making dinner in the kitchen. I walked right past her and went into the living room where Mark and Michelle were watching TV. I sat beside Michelle and asked her what had happened. She said Gloria wouldn't give them their family allowance cheques so that they could go buy jeans. I looked over to the kitchen and loudly asked Gloria, "Where's the kids' allowance?"

"It's up to your Dad to give it to them and he's not home, so I put it away 'til he gets here."

"Give them the cheques!"

"No."

"You're a fat fucking pig! This isn't your home!"

I suddenly heard the utility drawer open and the sound of Gloria's hand furiously searching for something. She came pounding towards me with a spatula in her hand and tried to slap me in the face with it. I batted it out of her hand and punched her in the mouth. She went for my hair and I grabbed her by the shirt, threw her on the couch, and started choking her. Michelle was yelling at me to stop while Mark stayed quiet. Dad suddenly came in. He saw us and said feebly, "Hey, c'mon, what are you doing, guys?" That brought me back to the reality of what I was doing, and I got off her. She sat up sputtering and yelling at Dad to call the police and get me out of the house. I stormed off to the kitchen while Gloria ran off to her bedroom.

I was shaking in bewilderment at what I had just done. Dad was unfazed by the whole scene, which says a lot about the tenor of the house at the time. "Dad, why does she have to keep the cheques?" I asked him, watching my back nervously. "They're not hers to control."

"You have to quit fighting and swearing," was his only reply.

A few minutes passed. Then there was a knock at the door. Gloria had called the police from her bedroom. Dad let the police in while I just sat silently on the couch. Gloria flew out of her bedroom like the cavalry had shown up to save her and demanded they take me away. An officer asked me what happened and my only reply was that she had asked for it. Gloria rattled on to the police about how I broke her dentures. "It's her or me," she told Dad.

From the living room I shouted, "Good, fucking go. No one wants you here anyway."

The police officer interjected, "Maybe you should leave until things cool down a bit."

"No, not until Dad tells me to. Dad?"

"Why do you got to swear so much?"

"It wasn't my swearing that started this! She's just like Mary all over again. I can't believe you're letting this happen again!"

"Julie, you swear too much."

"This is fucked! Have a good life with her. She better not mess with Mark or Michelle."

I went to Mom's to tell her what had happened. She couldn't stop laughing when I told her about cracking Gloria's dentures, but was concerned about the choking and Dad's lack of backbone.

Despite Gloria's ultimatum, I returned to Dad's once things cooled off. One weekend they left town to visit her parents and I decided to have a party. I called up some friends of my Uncle Ken and invited them over, telling them to bring as many people as they wanted. I didn't really consider the consequences of such an open invitation, but wasn't really worried about it—they wouldn't be back until Sunday and we'd be able to clean up by then.

Unfortunately, I had too much to drink, and things got out of hand. Someone started a fire right in the middle of the living room. The next morning I woke up to a huge burn mark on the floor and a dead bird, lying on the bottom of its cage, with its little feet curled up in the air. I'm not sure if it was the smoke or the loud music thumping below its cage that did it, but I knew that Gloria would not react well to the untimely death of her bird, Sweetheart. I had to call Gloria, and admittedly felt a touch of sadistic pleasure in doing so. I informed Gloria of the bird's demise and she dropped the phone, screaming out to Dad.

They came home and saw that the floor was burnt, the bird was dead, Gloria's bottles of tranquilizers were empty, and the locks on the house had been changed. "You'd better stop being so mean to Gloria, or you might break up the family," Dad scolded. I laughed, wondering, what family?

Through some combination of desperation to get out of Dad's house and blind escapism, I allowed myself to become involved with a gorgeous, but abusive boyfriend. Ed was a few years older than me: I was seventeen, he was twenty-three. Ed had his own body shop that was popular with guys who drove muscle cars. Metallic car paint was in and he had been the first to offer it in Regina. Things went smoothly for the first couple of months, but I did notice he had problems with me talking on the phone and visiting my mom alone. He would stare at me and listen to my conversations when I was on the phone. When I went to Mom's he would demand to know who else would be there. It seemed like little more than typical insecurity at the time, though it turned out to be much worse.

One night we were all hanging out at his house, listening to the new Boston record and smoking a joint. I made some comment about the singer's voice being a little high, and Ed snapped at me, "Who asked you?" A little surprised, I glanced over at his nephew Zeke with raised eyebrows, which I guess Ed took as a sign that something was going on between us. He seemed angry; his nostrils flared wildly. After everyone left I asked him if everything was okay.

"You have the hots for Zeke, don't you?"

"What? You're crazy."

He grabbed me around the throat and started to choke me.

"I saw you staring at him all night and then you gave him some kind of look! Don't lie, you fucking bitch!"

I tried to get him off me, pulling his hair and kicking him, all while it felt like my lungs were burning. I finally got my legs up and pushed him off. I sat there stunned at what had just happened. He immediately apologized and kept trying to kiss me. I started to cry and he held me tightly, swearing he'd never do that again. I said I wanted to go to Mom's and he said he would drive me. On the way I asked why he did that. His only reply was, "I don't want you to be with anyone else."

As we pulled up to Mom's house I saw the TV glaring through the window and was relieved someone was up. All I said to Ed was, "I'll call you tomorrow." He sped away as I ran into Mom's. I went in, sat down beside her, and told her what had happened. She seemed angry at me, which was Mom's way of being scared for me, and told me to break up with him. I wish I had listened to her that night, but I didn't.

I went downstairs to sleep in Sandy's room. In the dark I whispered to Sandy about what happened and Garnet, her new boyfriend, whom I thought had been sleeping, said, "If he's doing that now, Jules, he's not going to stop."

The next day I was helping Lisa babysit at her sister's house, when it occurred to me I hadn't called Ed yet. I thought I'd leave him to think for a while longer before I called. Wrong. We were sitting at the kitchen table when suddenly a foot came through the window. We both jumped up and I pulled back the curtain back to see Ed, yelling at me to get the fuck outside.

"What are you doing, you fucking idiot? Get lost!" I shouted.

"Fuck off!" Lisa added. Lisa's sister's kids started to cry because of all the shouting.

"Who the fuck is in there with you?" Ed demanded.

"Nobody. But so what if there was, what's it to you?" Lisa answered.

"Lise, fuck, are you nuts?" I muttered quietly.

"I'm going to call the cops!" she continued.

"Go ahead, bitch! I'll kill you when I see you again."

The neighbours came out to see what all the commotion was about and Ed told them to fuck off and mind their business. They went back inside, saying they were calling the cops. Ed took off, but not before threatening to kill us again.

"Lise, your sister is going to freak when she gets home. What are we going to do?"

"I have to tell her the truth. You probably shouldn't be here when I do."

"Okay. But what if he's waiting outside?"

"Call a cab and tell them to go around to the back of the house."

I called a cab, and then called Dad to see if he was home so he could pay for it. I told Dad I was having a boyfriend problem and needed to come home. He said okay, to my surprise. I nervously opened the door and ran out to see if the cab was there. Thank God it was. I got to Dad's hoping they wouldn't ask me too many questions. I was relieved that they didn't and that Gloria wasn't there to rub it in.

"If Ed calls, tell him you haven't seen me in a while," I told Dad before going downstairs to call Lisa. She said her sister was mad, and didn't want me around anymore. I said I'd pay for the window and asked her to call me back later. I lay on Mark's bed and put on an Aerosmith record. Mark came home and tried to cheer me up by inviting me to a party at our aunt's. I agreed, though I wasn't really in the mood. As I was heading out Gloria said, “You just got here! Why’d you make your Dad pay for the cab, then?”

I kept going and said, “I’ll be back in a while. Don’t lock the door.”

“We don’t leave our door unlocked around here. You never know who could walk in.”

I could have sworn that was directed at me. “They would take one look at you and run,” I said as I went out the door.

At the party I actually felt safer and less anxious about Ed turning up. I had never introduced Ed to Mom’s family and he had no idea where they lived. Everyone was drinking themselves silly and I was starting to feel a little better. I caught up with my cousin Luke and his girlfriend, Janice, who of course had already heard all about Ed from Mom’s sister.

“So who is this guy smacking you around?” Luke asked.

“He’s not smacking me around. We had an incident.”

“He was trying to choke you to death or something?”

“Yeah, well, it got a little crazy. I stopped talking to him, but then he came and kicked my friend’s window in.”

“Fuck, Jules, you desperate for a man or what?” Luke was always direct, and his words usually hit some truth.

“I don’t want to talk about it right now.”

“Yeah, leave her alone,” Janice chimed in.

“Okay, but if I hear about any more of his shit, Ed is gonna have to talk to the barrel of my gun.” I appreciated his concern, but laughed him off. I never expected things to escalate that far.

One night, after getting back together with Ed, we had an argument and I threatened to leave again. I was heading upstairs to get my things when I heard a gun being cocked behind me. I looked back and saw him pointing it at me. He fired just as I jumped away. If I hadn’t, he would have hit me. I ran for it, and he put the gun down and chased me down the street. He grabbed me by the hair, spun me around, and punched me in the mouth, splitting my lips. As soon as he saw the blood he freaked out and begged me not to leave him. His mom came outside and yelled, "Have you lost your mind? Let her go!"

I took off as fast I could, dripping blood and praying that he wouldn't catch me. I turned down a back alley, where a guy was out fixing his car. He looked at me and asked if I was okay.

"No, my boyfriend did this. I need to get to my mom's."

"Yeah, get in my car. Do you want to go to the hospital?"

"No, just my mom's. Thank you."

I lay down in the seat and thanked him profusely when we pulled up to the house. Mom and some of the guys from next door were barbequing and drinking beer, and they all freaked out when they saw me.

"What the fuck happened?" Mom demanded as she ran towards me.

"Ed."

"Get in the house and put some ice on that," she said as she waved her arms, stabbing the air with her fork.

From inside I heard the slamming of brakes on gravel as Ed pulled up, demanding I come outside. I heard Mom yell, "You get the fuck out of here before I stick this fork in your heart." He told her he had a gun in his car, and he'd blow her head off if she tried anything. One of the neighbours yelled that they had called the police and Ed took off as quickly as he'd arrived.

I was going to turn eighteen soon and I wanted to turn my life around. I wasn't happy with my friends or the things they were into. I no longer wanted to be around Mom's house or Dad's. I was sick of the chaos that both places created. I went and stayed with my Aunt Donalda and was happier drinking tea and playing cards with her. In exchange for letting me stay with her, I babysat for her and helped out around the house.

I started spending time with Donald, an old friend of my cousin Luke, who introduced me to a whole new group of friends. I met Dave when I went with Donald to pick him up from the doctor's; he'd been building a rocket and something had gone awry. He told us the whole story over coffee at Tastee Freeze and we hit it off immediately. He was hilarious, and a breath of fresh air compared to my old friends.

We'd hang out and watch Mork and Mindy and Saturday Night Live. I never missed an episode and loved how much safer it felt to be sitting with these cool new friends, without the fear of someone kicking in the door or getting into a fight. We just sat around smoking hash and playing pong. Sometimes we'd go out to Wascana and watch our friend Richard scale the Parliament Building, a stunt that earned him the nickname "Spiderman." I had such a good time with them and am thankful they helped me put my chaotic teenage years behind me.

Part Two:
From Calgary with Love
(1980s)

I was young when I fell in love with Bret—only twenty years old. I had spent those twenty years pretending to be a lot of people: the loner, the best friend, the stoner, the dropout, the runaway. I had been my father's daughter, until I wasn't. I had been my mother's daughter, until I wasn't. I was only a kid when I learned how to be a teenager, and I spent most of my teenage years learning how to be an adult. By the time I was twenty I had spent so much time dealing with adult problems like pregnancy and addiction that I pretty much assumed I was done with all the turmoil. But then I met Bret, and all the people I had pretended to be fell away. For the first time I was myself. I would later come to realize how closely my experience paralleled Bret's. Wrestling is a larger-than-life world of personas, and Bret had grown up in that world. Bret was the Hitman before he was the Hitman. He was the kid who stared bullies down when they threatened his sister. He was the kid who was always ready for a fight, even when he wasn't. Bret was like me—the kid who acted older than he was and grew up too fast because of it. But when I lay in his arms, neither of us was any of those people we had pretended to be. It was just him and me. I would go to bed feeling safe and happy, realizing I was young and in love.

Bret and I met at one of his matches in Regina. I was sitting up front, and apparently I caught his eye while he was in the ring. He asked my boss, Gil, who was running security for the event, to introduce us. Gil brought me to his dressing room, where we hung out and talked. I liked him right away, and couldn't wait for him to come back to town.

Bret was on the road all the time, but we met up whenever he came to Regina. In late December, Bret's brother Wayne called to tell me that Bret was going to be stopping in Regina for a show before returning home to Calgary for the holidays. Bret had been on the road for months and we hadn't spoken since he'd left. To say I was excited would be putting it mildly. My excitement, however, was tempered by my worry that he wouldn't be returning home alone. I was nervous that he had picked up a girlfriend while he was away or, worse still, a wife. I searched for ways to calm down and eventually settled on a serviceable way to channel my nervous energy: I went shopping.

I spent hours sorting through racks of acid-wash jeans and questionable hair products. Silly as it sounds, it kept my overactive imagination occupied long enough for me to relax. More importantly, it gave me a sense of control over a situation that felt increasingly out of my hands. I could present to Bret the version of myself I wanted him to see. I didn't know if he was single or attached, where he was with his career, or how long he would be staying in Regina. I didn't know if he had changed much, what he was really like, or if he was even still interested in me. What I did know was that when Bret got back, I was going to look good.

I went to work and asked Gil for an advance on my paycheque. After a big lecture on budgeting he finally gave in, and even drove me around as I looked for a new outfit. He seemed amused and confused each time I came out of a store empty handed. "Where to now, kiddo?" he'd say. I tried to explain that Bret had been really taken in by my sense of style, and that it was important for me to maintain my image. After all, there would be competition. It's always been about image with Bret, and I had known that right from the start. Gil laughed heartily and said, "Princess, all you have to do is flash 'em those pearly whites." I was like a daughter to Gil, and he never tried to hide it.

On the day of Bret's show I drove up to the auditorium with my heart pounding and my stomach doing flip-flops. I smoothed down my hair and went inside, hoping I wouldn't run into him without getting a covert glimpse of him first. I slipped into the dark arena as the first match was about to start. I saw my aunt sitting up front, but decided to stay in a more secluded spot. Maybe on some subconscious level I was making him wait to see me. Or better yet, maybe I wanted to see if he was standing in the shadows, looking to see if I was there. There I was, playing games from the very beginning. I went down a couple of rows to grab a program and check when Bret was up. He was on last, so decided I'd catch him after the show.

Feeling increasingly nervous, I moved up to the rafters and sat above the cheering and chanting of excited fans. I chuckled to myself as I watched old ladies yell expletives at the dreaded bad guys and shake with rage when their baby-faced wrestlers faked injuries. I have always marvelled at how these seemingly harmless grandmothers get so riled up over wrestling matches. My own grandmother hated Abdullah the Butcher so much that she had to be physically restrained when was in the ring. She was also so adamant that wrestling was real that she once almost got in a fist-fight with an old man who was shouting, "Chicken blood, blood capsules!" She was such a staunch believer that she got up, went down to the ring, wiped up some of the blood with her hand, and smeared it in the old man's face. This was, of course, in the early seventies, when matches always ended in bloodbaths.

During intermission I went down to chat with Gil, who was managing security for the show. I asked him if he had spoken with Bret, and he said just briefly. I raised my eyebrows and said, "Well, did he ask about me?"

"Nope."

I was crushed. "Hmm, I see. Do me a favour, Gil. Can you tell him I'm here and would like to see him when he's done? "

"For you, anything."

I was a little puzzled and went back up to the bleachers to obsess over things. I didn't really see much more of the wrestling. I kept watching the dressing room doors, waiting for Bret to appear. When he was introduced, the crowd went wild—his return had been heavily anticipated. I watched him as he jumped into the ring like a graceful cat. I checked out the hair; it looked good. He appeared to be a little bigger—not bad, I thought. The most noticeable thing was an increase in his confidence. He seemed less nervous and more agile. I think he was glad to be back. He'd always said Regina was his favourite place to wrestle, that the fans were different here. I waited in suspense for the match to end, not to see who would win, but so I could find out if Bret still wanted to see me. After the match Bret lingered by the ring, surrounded by a crowd of fans. Shoo, pesky flies, go away, I thought impatiently. I looked for Gil and saw him standing near the ring, smoking. Bret left with the crowd following him into the dressing room. I raced down the stairs to Gil. "Well?" I asked.

"Bret said wait here and he'll come out after he showers."

I was elated and sat down on the edge of the ring. Time moved slowly, and I found myself worrying about how I looked sitting there. Am I slouching too much? Am I not slouching enough? What is the proper way to slouch when waiting for someone? All of a sudden, he floated towards me. I was speechless. I had forgotten the fullness of his lips and the colour of his eyes, which seemed brighter than I remembered. We both nervously said, "Hi." Then from out of nowhere, with a mix of assertiveness and insecurity, I said, "So is this it?"

"What do you mean?"

"Do you still want to see me or not?"

"Yes, I do," he said, looking amused at my abruptness. I felt a sudden rush of feelings, like what I imagined love felt like.

After that night Bret and I carried on a weekly romance. We saw each other once a week for just a few minutes after each show—a quick kiss and a passionate hug. Gil would sometimes let us sit in his van for the few short minutes we had. I felt like a schoolgirl and sighed heavily into the phone when he called. I was restless and moody, like the world didn't exist until he called me. I tried to occupy myself with work and reading, faithfully buying

Rolling Stone and working overtime. I loved the way he held me when we finally saw each other, his strong arms conveying how he felt without a single word.

Some weeks I brought Michelle along to the shows. Bret developed a soft spot for Michelle the moment he met her. He treated her like a little sister and she loved every minute of it. I was a little apprehensive about taking Bret home to meet the rest of my family. When I found out he would be staying a night in Regina, I invited him to stay at my mom's. Part of me was hoping he would say no, but he happily agreed. I made my mom clean the house and even lectured the kids on manners.

My room was in the basement, and I cleaned it as though I were expecting royalty. I put all of my favourite albums in front of the stereo for easy access. When he arrived in Regina I tried to keep him out as late as I could, hoping the kids would be in bed by the time we got home. Fat chance. After quickly introducing him to everyone, I dragged him to my room, where we spent the night talking and listening to music. Beneath a thick layer of blankets and Van Morrison, Bret and I said I love you to each other—eventually. It started rather awkwardly, with us playfully joking around about who would be the first to say it. I tried to make him say it first, but we both giggled and muffled our words into the blanket. There was a lot of "So, ahh…I…okay…you know, I think I…" After a few minutes of this, Bret bravely professed his love for me, and I did the same.

The next morning I woke up late for work. Gil was outside waiting to give me a ride and honking his horn like crazy. I ran out and asked him to give me ten minutes. He said I had five. I raced back into the house, flew down the stairs, and jumped back into bed with Bret. I kept repeating, "I love you," and he kept saying it too. Returning to Gil's van, I looked back at the house and exclaimed, "I forgot my mitts!" I jumped back in the bed, and we exchanged another round of hasty I love you's. After going back inside a final time to retrieve my hat, Gil and I took off for work.

Gil was neither angry nor surprised by the delay; he had spotted the Alberta license plates in the driveway and asked if I had company. I looked at him with a smile and nodded. He warned me to be careful. "You don't really know this guy, Princess, and I don't want to see you get hurt." I didn't take his words as meaningful advice, but rather as criticism of Bret. "What do you mean by that?" I snapped back.

"Well, he's on the road a lot, and you might not be the only one he's stopping in for."

"Bret's not like that. He's shy and sensitive."

"Look, I know what goes on, on the road and off the road. There are many spots in between, if you get what I mean." Gil knew what he was talking about. He used to wrestle with Bret's father. We drove in silence the rest of the way to work.

Bret hit the road again and I grew anxious imagining what he was up to. I wondered whether our relationship could survive the long distance. I could hardly wait for his Sunday phone calls. The only picture I had of him was from a wrestling program. I wore that black-and-white picture out and carefully folded it so as not to crease his face. I wouldn't have dreamt of asking him for another one. During his interview on a Saturday-afternoon broadcast, I watched his mouth and thought about kissing it. Wow—what a mark!—but it was all I had.

I suppose he missed me, too, because the next time he called he invited me to visit him in Calgary. When I went the following weekend he took me around and showed me all of the schools he had gone to. It meant something to him for me to sit outside of those buildings with him, listening to his stories of fights and embarrassing moments. Bret always had to defend himself and his siblings from bullies and, occasionally, his other siblings. I sympathized with him because I felt like I had spent my life defending others.

Our relationship took off from there and before I knew it I was moving to Calgary. I arrived to an empty house—Bret was at a match and had told me to wait there for him to come home. I walked around the house, discovering that it was a typical guy's place, with *Playboy* bunnies showcased proudly in the bathroom. The house had an unusual layout: It was like a barn, and the floors sloped up and down like a game of chutes and ladders. It was a good size, but, as I would soon find out, nothing like the Hart family's sprawling, opulent home. Bret's home reminded me more of Regina. It was in a poorer neighbourhood, with grassless yards and crowded lots. I think he was trying to deny his silver spoon, and that he felt better struggling on his own. It was all so new it made me a little uncomfortable, but it wasn't like I had never left home before.

Things got off to a rough start. I felt overwhelmed and couldn't find the nerve to do the simplest things, like cook for Bret or go to his parents' for their big Sunday dinners. I just felt too intimidated by them. This upset Bret, but he was willing to give me some time to adjust and went on eating his bachelor meals for the first few weeks. It was probably for the best—he was training, and his diet seemed incredibly demanding. He'd fry up four eggs at a time and scarf down half a package of bacon as though it was nothing. For dinner it'd be milkshakes and fish sticks or whole chickens. I've quite never gotten over the sight of him eating an avocado like it was an apple. Eventually I settled down and my insecurities faded. Bret and I spent our time together listening to music and making plans for our future. Sometimes we'd play each other our favourite songs, letting the lyrics speak for us. I found my life to be perfect in those moments. I was in love and everything was magical and exciting. Bret witnessed all the silly things a girl does when she feels that way: I wore his shirts, made sure my legs were always stubble-free, and kept my teeth sparkling white. I held him at night as we lay in bed with the windows open, the cool breeze carrying our promises of love through the air.

I was still trying to avoid dinner at the Hart house, but Bret eventually got tired of my games, and so one Sunday we finally headed over. It was now mid-May, and the sun beat down on us as Bret and I approached the house. The surrounding neighbourhood was quiet and filled with comfortable-looking houses. There were a few joggers doing their ritual and a few families making their way to the park, but for the most part the sidewalks were empty. The Hart house itself was big, and when I say big, I mean twenty-two rooms, four fireplaces, and five chandeliers big. But it wasn't just the size of the house that intimidated me. Anyone familiar with Canadian wrestling knows about the Hart house. Bret's father, Stu, was the founder of Stampede Wrestling, a major promotion company in Calgary, and he trained many of his wrestlers there. The home boasted a training studio in the basement known as "The Dungeon." Many of Canada's greatest wrestlers have passed through the Dungeon, including Davey Boy Smith, Chris Jericho, Lance Storm and Chris Benoit. There is a lot of history in the Hart house, especially for Bret and his siblings, all of whom either became wrestlers or married wrestlers. As we walked up the front steps I remember thinking to myself, we haven't even stepped inside, and I already feel out of place.

The intimidation I felt on the way there immediately faded when I met Bret's mom, Helen. Born and raised in Long Island, Helen was exactly as Bret described her: a small woman of grand stature. I'll never forget how she gently took my hand and, in that charming New York accent, said, "Oh, hello, dahling, I'm so happy to meet you." Helen's sense of humour made me relax instantly. She was sweet, witty, and always sure to include you in the jokes. Of course, after Helen came Stu. I stood rather awkwardly in the foyer, waiting for the big guy to approach me. Stu had a towel flung over his shoulder and put his hand out for me to shake, but also, in a rather quick swoop of his baby blue eyes, gave me the once over. His eyes focused on my teeth and legs. I was being checked out like a thoroughbred horse. Good teeth and long legs were Stu's measurement of a girl. Bret and I went outside and watched his brothers and a couple of girls toss the football around.

"Ehhh, you're from Regina then?" Stu scratched out with his trademark growl.

"Yes, born and raised a diehard Roughrider fan," I offered, hoping to connect with Stu by bringing up Regina's CFL team.

"Gad-dah, I played for the Edmonton Eskimos in 1938 and 1939. I remember when big Gene Kiniski played for them. Gad…he was a big bastard, and he had a helluva set of cauliflower ears on him."

Helen was quick to cut him off before he could go any further down memory lane. "Stu, Julie doesn't want to hear about old wrestlers."

Helen led me into the living room, away from the men. I heard Stu say, "Gad, Tiger Balls is a little miffed." Stu had nicknamed Helen "Tiger Belle" and, depending on the severity of the swipes she gave him, the name often morphed into "Tiger Balls."

"Sorry, dahling. Stu has a tendency to take any topic of conversation and relate it to wrestling. When he asks for directions, he asks where the nearest arena is and takes it from there," Helen apologized with her girlish laugh.

We eventually all sat down to eat. The dinner itself will forever remain etched my memory, and I still laugh whenever someone brings it up. The table was crowded with an impossible amount of food and, figuring I should pace myself, I passed on the salad when it came my way. This did not go unnoticed by Bret's sister Ellie, who was pregnant at the time and had never been one to hide her feelings. "Too good for the fucking salad?" she sneered from across the table. Her comment left me speechless. Bret and I stood up to make our exit. Bret's sister Georgia caught up with us outside and was quick to blame Ellie's pregnancy for her behaviour, but Bret wouldn't let Ellie off the hook. Ellie had always been the most vocal of the Harts and you have to admire her for that. Over the years I came to adore her. She had a great sense of style and was very artistic, like all of the Hart girls. Diana was especially gifted at drawing and was athletic to boot. Georgia was an incredible cook whose culinary talents outdid even Stu's legendary skill with prime rib. Alison had a sharp political mind and was very literary, like her mother. The whole family was all so wonderful and talented, as well as being just damn funny. Owen in particular had a great, teasing sense of humour that I would later come to recognize in my daughter Beans.

Bret went to Japan for a few weeks to wrestle as a tag team with his brother Keith, leaving me alone in Calgary for the first time. I got lonely and spent a lot of time with Keith's girlfriend, Leslie. One night while we were chatting, she "smartened me up to the biz." She told me what "kayfabe" meant, explaining it referred to the illusion the wrestlers were trying to keep up. She added that, "If you walk into a room while the guys are talking, and one of them says 'kayfabe,' he is telling the other guys to keep quiet about something." I was shocked and upset at the secrecy of it, feeling as though I was being personally deceived.

When Bret called I could tell how homesick he was. He kept talking about how much longer he had to go and how he couldn't wait to see me. I blurted out, "Leslie told me everything about wrestling—why didn't you tell me?" He was caught off guard and couldn't understand why I was upset. The call ended with me hanging up and saying I was out of here.

The next day his brother Bruce showed up to ask how I was doing. He said I shouldn't be feeling the way I was and that it was just the nature of the business—it had nothing to do with me personally. He joked around with me and had me laughing so hard that it was tough not to feel silly about being "kayfabed." I felt better, but then worse about how I had acted with Bret. I had no idea how to get a hold of him and panicked over my impulsive behaviour. Thankfully, Bret had already forgiven me by the time I reached him. I wish I could take back those many out-of-control moments.

I now feel truly sorry for how I behaved then, and at other times like it. I was immature, and trying to push before being shoved.

For Christmas Bret got me a promise ring. I adored it and still do, even though these days most women would scoff at such a tiny chip of diamond. Today it's all about the zing in the bling. It meant the world to me, despite the number of times I hurled it back at him during our juvenile arguments. Michelle's love life was also getting interesting; Tom Billington, a wrestler from England who had been recruited by Stu, had developed an interest in her, making both Bret and me very nervous. Tom's unique, highflying style had been making waves overseas. Though he was smaller than most, the crowds here were beginning to take an interest in the newcomer.

When Bret and I talked about our future together, it always seemed like a distant promise. Then I got pregnant and we had to decide if we were ready for a family. I knew deep down that neither of us was ready for parenthood. Bret's career was struggling and he worried about money constantly. Wrestling was an incredibly capricious business. Most of Stu's boys had gone to Japan that summer to make money. They were all working so hard, especially Stu. He was like a father to all of his wrestlers, always taking their phone calls and hearing out their problems, both professional and personal.

We agreed that it wasn't the right time to have a baby. Abortion is an extremely difficult decision to make, but we had neither the time nor the money to raise a child. I put on a mask of acceptance, but was deeply saddened by my choice. I never really expressed my misgivings about it to Bret; he seemed relieved that I wasn't making a fuss over it, and I didn't want to make the situation worse.

Soon after, Bret asked me to join him on a trip overseas. I think he'd noticed that I was feeling depressed about our decision and wanted to cheer me up. I couldn't refuse. Bret was a great person to travel with; it really brought out his sense of adventure. We started in Germany, where he and Jim Neidhart had a wrestling gig. Wrestling was different in Germany; it was more gimmicky and very crooked. Referees would fine the wrestlers, who would then appeal to the fans for money to pay them. I felt sorry for the poor, unassuming fans who would pay the fines, not realizing that the referees and wrestlers split the money at the end of the night. One of the most outrageous wrestlers was Adrian Street. His gimmick was to act like a flamboyant gay man, and the fans loved it. Every night he received flowers, women's shoes, and money from men. I had a bit of a crush on one of the referees, a dark Frenchman named Didi, who looked like a film star from the thirties. I was often more interested in watching him than the wrestling.

We were staying with Bret's friend Jochim and his wife, Heidi, whom I became fast friends with. For the first few nights there I hung out with Heidi while Jochim took Bret and Jim out on the town. Jochim was a cop, so he knew the ins and outs of all the seediest places in the city. They would come home with the craziest stories, and it made me want to go out too. So on their next night out, I tagged along. Their stories weren't exaggerations. We went to brothels and live sex shows, which shocked me, even though I had known what to expect. One of the brothels had baby tigers and lions and torture rooms. I was given a mask and a whip by the madame and Bret was put on a stretching table. Jim even got a turn whipping Bret!

The trip wasn't all fun and games, though. One night, one of Jochim's friends had too much to drink and started hitting on Bret right in front of me. She put her hand on his leg and started rubbing it, so I grabbed her hand and threw it off. I got in her face about it and Bret just sat there laughing. He thought the whole situation was amusing, but I found their behaviour to be plain disrespectful. I was furious and said I wanted to leave. Jochim drove us back to his place, and as we approached the house I started mouthing off to Bret. Suddenly, he bodyslammed me into a flowerbed. He knocked the wind out of me so badly I couldn't get up. He offered me a hand, but I told him to fuck off and just lay in the flowers as he walked away.

I was still angry about that night when, a few days later, Bret came home from a night out smelling like perfume. I snapped. I grabbed him by the head and dug my fingernails into his face and eyes. Bret has always said he never saw me in the same way after that.

We left for England and things seemed to improve with the change of scenery. Michelle and Tom were there as well, which cheered me up. Tom had gotten Bret booked with a British promotion company called Max Crabtree's. Bret was a little disappointed when he found out his ring name: "Cowboy Bret Hart." I thought it was Tom's idea of a joke, but apparently the English fans were mad for anything to do with cowboys. Tom said they watched too many Westerns and thought everyone in Canada still rode around on horses. Bret had to wear a big, black cowboy hat and play the bad guy.

When he wasn't playing cowboy, Bret came sightseeing with me, accommodating my every whim. We went to see musicals in the old theatres. We went to Hyde Park, and then Buckingham Palace, where we held hands in the rain without saying a word. When Bret and Tom went on the road, Michelle and I did our own tour of England. Tom warned us to not act like daft tourists when we said we were going to go to Liverpool to check out the home of the Beatles. Michelle and I also visited historic graveyards, and were surprised by how old the headsrones were. We had so much fun exploring England.

When we got back to Calgary, Michelle and Tom continued to fall deeper in love. At the time, Tom and Bret were having some of the best matches in Calgary, and I found it a bit uncanny that my sister and I were their partners behind the scenes. A few months later, Michelle and Tom got married. I was happy for them, but thought it was too soon and that she was too young. I was one to talk. I had just turned twenty-two on their wedding day, and already felt like Bret's wife. I enjoyed taking care of him and making sure the house was perfect for him when he came home off the road. I remember the

Sandy and me as a baby.

Sandy, Mark, Michelle and me.

Mom and Dad.

With Bret.

With Bret overseas.

Bret and Dallas.

Me in the 80s.

Photo credit: Randy Hill

Pink and Black attack.

Jade and Miss Elizabeth.

With Brian Knobbs and Bill Goldberg during Bret's WCW days.

Owen and Martha's wedding.

The kids at Survivor Series in 1994.

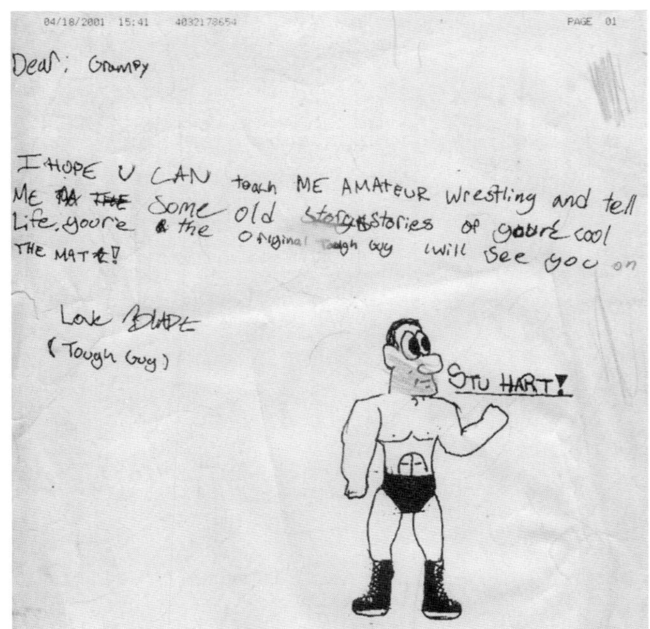

04/18/2001 15:41 4032178654 PAGE 01

Dear: Grampy

I HOPE U CAN teach ME AMATEUR wrestling and tell ME Some old stories of youre cool Life, youre the Original Tough Guy I will See you on THE MAT!

Love BLADE
(Tough Guy)

STU HART!

A drawing Blade made for Stu when he was sick.

With my dear friend Colleen.

With Michelle.

With Wayne Gretzky and Bret.

Photo credit: Ashid Bahl

At Machu Picchu.

Photo credit: Bill Brooks/Calgary Sun

The last picture of Bret and me together.

Photo credit: Randy Hill

The kids' favorite family picture. Mine too.

excitement I felt when he would walk through the door and come up behind me and kiss my neck, or spin me around for a passionate kiss.

When Bret and I got married it was quick and secret. Bret didn't want his family to know and said most of them didn't deserve to know. We actually saw ourselves as relatively private people and weren't comfortable with the idea of a big ceremony. I made all of the arrangements for the "big M," as we covertly called it. Bret seemed so unconcerned with it all that I didn't even expect him to have a ring.

We were married on July 8th, 1982. On the morning of the wedding, we found out that we needed two witnesses, so we called our friend Dean Wilkinson and asked him to be one of them. Thinking quickly, we ran across the street to the pizza place that was owned by our friend George Galantis, scooped him up, and headed to the Calgary courthouse. It was a quick process: we signed the papers, said our vows, and when the official asked if we were exchanging rings, we both said no. We rushed outside and, on the courthouse steps, Bret gave me my ring. It was a puzzle ring and he had a matching one — which he would never wear. Our wedding reception was held at George's restaurant. I had baked lasagna and Bret had the ribs. It lasted a whole hour, then Bret had to rush off and wrestle. "I promise, Jules, someday we'll have the kind of wedding you want."

I became pregnant with Jade on Bret's birthday. I just knew she had been conceived—it was the strangest of feelings. I was soon bursting at the seams, wanting to tell everyone of my joy, but Bret forbade it, wanting to wait. I kept dropping hints and teasing Michelle about having big news. Eventually I told Bret I didn't want to wait anymore. Besides, after five months I was starting to show. I flew out the door when he said I could tell Michelle. I had to get her to promise not to tell anyone else. Bret wanted to write Stu and Helen a letter explaining things. It hurt me that he didn't want to tell them face to face. He put the letter under his mom's pillow the night before they left for a trip to the States, as though he wanted to avoid a confrontation. He'd always said that his parents wanted their kids to marry the best, which meant someone with a name, money, and most importantly, an education. I didn't have any of those.

Jade Michelle Koo Hart was born March 31, 1982. The "Koo" came from Bret's fascination with Prince Andrew's erotic-filmstar girlfriend. I didn't mind as long as my sister Michelle's name also adorned the birth certificate. I must have been the most nervous new mother ever. On the day I was to take Jade home, away from the safety of the nursery, I couldn't stop envisioning myself dropping her on her head. The nurses laughed and assured me that it was normal to be anxious, and that my instincts would kick in soon enough. Bret picked me up from the hospital, and as we drove home I clutched Jade like a baby doll.

We instantly fell in love with Jade. We'd spend hours staring at her, captivated by her pleasant disposition. Her hair was curly and her eyes were as big and brown as a baby fawn's. She adapted so easily to our crazy lifestyle. Most nights she'd sleep quietly between Bret and me in our bed. On nights when Bret got home late she'd be up until the craziest hours waiting for him.

Helen and Stu often babysat for us so that we could go out for dinner or catch a movie. When we went to pick Jade up she'd always be fast asleep in an old-fashioned baby carriage. Stu would be sitting on the couch with his hands behind his head—a familiar Hart pose—and Helen on his lap. There would be tea brewing for us. It was always picture perfect.

During those first few months, Helen proved to be a constant source of comfort and reassurance. I remember calling her, distraught that I couldn't breastfeed. With her ever-present wit and charm, she simply replied, "Does Jade have all ten fingers and toes, dahling?" She always had me laughing with stories about her first time being a mother.

When she was old enough I took Jade to Regina so everyone could see her. I barely saw her the whole time we were there—everyone took turns taking care of her and sleeping with her. All they wanted to do was keep her happy; I don't remember hearing her cry a single time during the trip.

A year later I became pregnant again, and this time Bret was a little upset that I hadn't been more careful. The wrestling business was struggling more than ever, and he was worried about being able to provide for a bigger family. The lucrative trips to Japan were becoming scarcer. There were also rumours that Vince McMahon was going to buy up the smaller territories, or worse, just take them over. Bret was afraid his father would lose everything he had worked so hard for, which added personal stress to the financial anxiety.

Between his stress and my hormones, Bret and I grew distant. During the pregnancy everyone seemed to annoy me, especially him. It didn't help that the pregnancy was an extremely painful one; the baby's slightest movements would often cause me unbearable pain.

On the night I went into labour Bret was out with some radio disc jockey from Vancouver. I remember asking him not to go because I was due with Dallas any day. Perhaps fed up with me over all my erratic behavior, he yelled, "I will go where I want, when I want," and left, slamming the door behind him. I stood there stunned until the martyr in me kicked in—then I ran to the door and yelled obscenities at him as he drove away. Later that night, as I lay in bed with Jade, my water broke. I got up and went to check the other rooms to see if Bret was sleeping on a couch. He hadn't come home yet. It was quite late and I needed to get to the hospital. I called Michelle, but she had her own four-month-old baby, Bronwyne, to look after and couldn't leave. I tried our friend Dean next. He asked where Bret was and I said I didn't know. Dean drove from the other end of the city and made it to my house in twenty minutes. I had already jumped in the old gray caddie and driven myself to the hospital. It was a long, lonely labour. Michelle showed up early in the morning, having left Bronwyne with a friend. I had Dallas several hours later, at around six in the evening. I was so furious with Bret I thought of divorcing him. I was tired of him being so unsupportive, and I didn't see how things were going to change.

Dallas looked like Yoda from *Star Wars*. He had thin wisps of blonde hair on top of his tiny head and a bad case of jaundice. He had to be kept under special lights because of it, and was well tanned by the time we brought him home. He was a quiet, happy baby who gained weight at an unbelievable rate. When he started teething we nicknamed him "Bear" because he would put his entire fist in mouth and gnaw on it ferociously. Even his teeth turned out to be enormous—they were like Chiclets. No wonder he had such a rough time teething.

The two children kept me occupied while Bret focused on making it into the WWF. Stu had made a deal with Vince McMahon, in which Vince agreed to take Tom and Bret. I don't think Vince wanted either of them, really, but he agreed out of respect for Stu and old-school handshakes. Bret came home from a meeting with the WWF people and informed me that if he signed on with them, he'd be gone for six to eight weeks at a time. I knew I was about to understand what sacrifice meant for us. The trips to Japan had only been for six weeks, twice a year. When Bret wrestled around Calgary he was always within driving distance, with the occasional overnight trip. We knew it would be tough, and a true test of the strength of our marriage. Bret likened it to a soldier going off to war, hopefully to return home victorious, having won a better future for his children.

Bret's first few years in the WWF were a rollercoaster ride. He had many supporters, but there were also many people who didn't believe in his talent. It was heartbreaking to hear him so discouraged when he came off the road. He began to doubt his ability because he was never given any chances to prove himself.

Between my loneliness and his self-doubt, our marriage suffered. We both silently hoped that we could hang on, and that the sacrifices would pay off. Bret would always tell me to hold on because "in the end, I'm coming home to you and the kids." I gained a brighter perspective on everything when I saw my first WWF show in Toronto. I felt so proud seeing him wrestle in such a big arena.

Bret got fed up with the neighbourhood we were living in and decided it was time to go. Tom and Michelle had us move in with them until we found a new place. Tom liked the idea of Michelle and I keeping each other company while he and Bret were on the road, and also loved it when we were all there under one roof. When Bret and I eventually found a townhouse near the Hart house, I was a little sad to leave.

When Bret called me from the road, all he could talk about was how lonely he was. That, along with his increasing popularity, began to worry me. It wasn't long before I found out about the girl from New Jersey. I had a rather sudden itch that wouldn't go away. I went to see a doctor, and when he told me what I had I assumed I'd picked it up from some public bathroom. When I got home I stripped the beds and threw every piece of laundry I had into garbage bags. As soon as I calmed down, my suspicions rose. I took out our phone bills. I was surprised to see that Bret had spent more hours calling some number in New Jersey than home. There was someone else, and I had the body lice and long-distance calls to prove it. Just to be sure, I went through the receipts that Bret was so meticulous about keeping. Silly boy, he even kept the bill for an expensive red sweater he bought her for Christmas.

I sat in the middle of the living room floor and started crying. The kids came into the room, confused, and I snapped at them to go to their rooms. I called my friend Wanda to tell her about my discoveries. I ranted and raved and she said she'd come right over. She found me still sitting on the floor and came over and hugged me. She said it was typically selfish of him, while I blamed myself for being so blind and stupid. I felt like I should have listened to all the people who tried to warn me over the years.

Two days later Bret called from Albuquerque. "I want a divorce!" I screamed, before he even had a chance to ask how I was. I hung up the phone and unplugged it so I wouldn't have to hear his lies. He called the next day and begged me to meet him in Minneapolis. I said no, but he kept calling. I asked Wanda to watch the kids and flew to the States the next day.

I met Bret at an arena and as we walked to the rental car I started mouthing off about his new girl. He stopped and I continued walking. Suddenly, Bret flung a can of Budweiser at me, hitting me on the head. I swung around and charged at him with my purse. Les Thorton, the wrestler, crossed the parking lot and got in the middle of us. I declared that I wasn't getting in a car with Bret. Bret angrily yelled, "Shut the fuck up and get in the car and stop embarrassing yourself." Les chimed in, "Come on, love, I think you two should talk." I stubbornly said no, but soon found myself sitting in the car.

When we got back to the hotel room, some girl called, asking for Bret. I lost it and hurled a lamp at him. It fell to the ground and smashed to pieces. Silence overcame me and I just sat there, listening to him explain that the girl meant nothing to him and that I should be thankful he wasn't hooked on pills or coke like the other boys.

I decided to stay with him, but nothing was the same with us after the affair. I tried my best to trust him again and he tried his best to convince me he was faithful.

A few months after I confronted Bret with his infidelity my grandmother died. I was devastated. I went home for the funeral, taking the kids with me. Bret phoned to check in with me every few days, but I couldn't have cared less about the calls. Everyone kept telling me how lucky I was and asking me about my fabulous life. If only they knew.

With everything going so badly, drugs became a bigger part of our lifestyle. Bret and I would do them together, and dabble just as much on our own. Our trip to the dreaded state of New Jersey was a coke-filled nightmare. The drugs helped me not think about Bret and what had happened in that state. I would do coke and sleep in the car, just to escape Bret and the painful thoughts he inspired. Every time I thought about the affair, I would ask him for more.

Our lives began to turn around when Vince started drug testing the boys. Too many of them were getting messed up on coke. They would get high all the time, and then take Halcions and sleeping pills to bring themselves down. Wrestling was becoming wildly popular thanks to stars like Terry Bollea, aka Hulk Hogan, and Vince had to get his boys under control. If anyone could do it, it was Vince. With his booming voice and intimidating manner, he always reminded me of a customs agent who could make you feel guilty even if you hadn't done anything wrong.

Vince intimidated me from the first moment I saw him. He was wearing an expensive suit with suede running shoes. Thinking it was kind of weird, I asked Bret about it.

"Why is he wearing running shoes?"

"So that he can go back and forth."

During the matches, he'd be all over the place, doing commentary, running through the dressing rooms, and dealing with office stuff. The shoes were almost like his little signature. He had his quirks, but he was in control. I thought he was brilliant, and still do. I don't think there is wrestling fan on the planet who doesn't know that Vince changed wrestling forever. And he did a pretty damn good job of it. I don't know Vince McMahon from a fan's perspective; I know Vince McMahon as the person who gave us what he did. Our family did well because of Vince. My kids and I had everything. I got to travel, and was one of the first wives to actually go overseas with the boys. It didn't happen in those days because they didn't want the wives around; the boys couldn't be themselves that way. My first trip was to Japan, and I remember Bret saying that it was unheard of, that it was so nice of Vince to let me tag along. When I saw Vince at the airport before we left, I went up to him and said, "Vince, thank you, I am so grateful, thank you," but I didn't look him in the eyes. I kept looking away because he really was bigger than life. It's the same way people look at Hulk Hogan.

Vince didn't quite get rid of all the drugs, and I found that out the hard way at my first WrestleMania in Chicago. The night started out innocently enough, with me bumping into my childhood heavy-metal hero, Ozzy Osbourne, backstage. I was so pleased to meet him, I couldn't help but "mark out," as we say in the wrestling world, when fans go crazy for their idols. I went back to my seat and gleefully watched Ozzy pretend to be the Bulldog's manager. After the show we all went back to the hotel for drinks. Tom was in rare form and, as a prank, pilled my drink. I didn't notice until I went to the bathroom and couldn't stand up. I ripped my nylons at the knees in my struggle to get back up and out of the bathroom. Tom just kept laughing at me, pointing at the holes in my nylons and calling me daft. I might have been embarrassed if I had been conscious enough to care.

As the kids got older, we started traveling as a family more. The kids loved being around all the wrestlers, who acted like big brothers. They would play with them and make them feel safe and at home while on the road. They were always so polite in front of me and the kids. No swearing around women—it was part of a code that the Southern boys passed on to everyone. I swapped stories with the other wives and received a lot of support and encouragement from them. There was also plenty for us to explore outside of the arenas. I especially loved getting dressed up with Jade and taking her to Broadway shows. Whenever we went out for a family dinner, the kids would be on their silliest behaviour. Fans would come up to ask for pictures and Dallas would always try to steal the spotlight and mug for the camera.

All of the little holidays and trips out to see him wrestle were Bret's way of making up for his absence at home. He also made sure the kids had all the latest toys. He would drag himself around the toy stores, looking for the most popular *Ghostbusters* toys for Dallas. Jade had every Gem doll and a handcrafted house to keep them in. He was very good at keeping the kids happy, but I still wish he could have made it to more Christmas plays and big games. I began to resent wrestling and wished more than anything for Bret to quit. We had a big new house with an Olympic-style pool, but it always felt empty without him. I felt ungrateful and guilty, but I just wanted us to be a normal family.

I experienced a lot of boredom and loneliness when Bret was on the road. The more success Bret saw, the less time he had for his family. His success also made it harder for me to make real friends. Everyone was dying to be my friend just to get closer to "The Hitman." There were a select few from the Stampede days whom I could count as true friends. Everyone else just wanted to throw my name around like it was a quarter to get special privileges. I suppose that kind of thing was good for the clubs or discount carpets.

To make things worse, when Bret got home all he wanted was peace and quiet. He hated having people hanging around the house and never wanted to host parties. His favorite slogan was "in by four, out by six." I could always count on my sisters for a good time, though. I spent many nights out with my sister Elaine, watching her boyfriend's band play all over Calgary. I always had a great time with them and met some wonderful new friends. It was refreshing to step completely out of Bret's world, however briefly.

Even with Bret on the road all the time, the house was about to feel a little less empty. I was pregnant again. Bret was always proud of how I looked when I was pregnant; he'd comment on my "glow" and brag about how great I looked. I was happier this time around and felt supported by my family. Early on Sandy declared that she wanted to be the first person to see the baby, and she was right there in the delivery room for the birth of Beans. Stu came up to see Beans when she was born and said how her hands were a combination of his and Helen's hands. He said, "with hands like that, she'll go far." Beans was a beautiful baby with soft blonde hair and big blue eyes.

Sometimes Bret would return home and bring the craziness of the road back with him. One night, when the WWF was in Calgary, we threw a dinner party and invited some of the wrestlers, including Harley Race, who was Tom's best friend. As the party carried into the night, we ran out of ice, and so Harley drove Michelle and me to the store. It was winter and really icy on the roads, but Harley just slammed Michelle's Bronco into four-wheel drive and said, "I'm going to show you how to drive!" Oh my God, what a ride. It was the scariest five minutes of my life.

When we got to the store, Michelle and I grabbed a bag of ice, which was frozen into one giant, solid block. Back home, Harley took one look at the block of ice and just said, "Give me that Big Sweet." He grabbed the bag and punched it, and the whole block shattered! Later someone whispered to me, "Nobody likes to shake Harley's hand because he's got the strongest tendons ever known to anyone. He could break your hand with just a handshake. Everyone always shakes his hand really gently, and never the whole hand."

Part Three: *The Roaring 1990s*

In June of 1990, we welcomed Blade Colton Hart into the world. He looked exactly like Bret did when he was a baby. His eyes were black as coal and he had thick brown hair. He became our golden child. After he was born, we decided we were finished having kids. We now had our perfect little set of four cubs.

A few months later, Bret's brother Dean died of a kidney disease he had been fighting for years. All we wanted to do was stop and mourn, but unfortunately that wasn't exactly possible. I remember watching Bret in the Survivor Series pay-per-view the night after Dean died, wondering how he could do it. By all accounts, Dean was Bret's idol growing up. I could see in the Hitman's eyes that he was trying not to think of Dean as he wrestled. He had a lost look as he worked through his match. He was devastated, but the show had to go on.

Bret and Dean had been inseparable when they were younger. Bret would tell me stories of their childhood, and it seemed he learned more from Dean than anyone. Dean showed Bret how to use his imagination, and how to turn what he imagined into a living dream. I suppose growing up on the outskirts of Calgary forced you to rely on your imagination to pass the time.

I had always been fond of Dean and always said that he and Bruce were the handsomest of the Hart boys. Dean looked like a cherub, with big, round eyes and loose curls of brown hair. I could see why Helen and Stu adored him. The first time I met Dean was during a Hart family Sunday dinner. I was standing on the veranda, watching the boys play football. I kept my eye on the smaller, well-tanned guy throwing the ball and running like hell in his cut-off jean shorts. I didn't know it was Dean at the time. Stu rang a bell, calling us in to eat, and I waited on the veranda for Bret to come up before going in. As Bret walked up the stairs,

Dean passed right by him and came directly over to me. "Hi, I'm Dean Hart." His eyes and teeth looked so bright when he smiled that I lowered my gaze because of how beautiful he really was. Bret came over to introduce us, but saw from my shyness that I had already met Dean.

The last time I talked with Dean was a few weeks before he passed in November. He brought over a board game he knew Bret loved to play. Dean was pale and thin from dialysis by then, and quite stubborn about taking any medical advice. I suppose he was in denial more than anything. I can only imagine the pain he must have been feeling. Once Bret returned from Survivor Series, the Harts held the funeral. Owen was in Germany and sent a tape expressing his feelings about his brother. The rest of the family gave eulogies as well. Smith's words about finding his brother on the day he died were spoken with such anguish that the entire room was unsure of how to react. Helen was so overwrought with grief that she hardly spoke a word. Dean was remembered as a fighter until the very end.

The nineties was a wild decade, with Bret in the midst of his major push towards the WWF's top tier. We were partying more than ever, him on the road and me back in Calgary. I'd become friends with an amazing band, Smash L.A., and was getting caught up in their lifestyle. Their guitarist, Marc, became like a little brother to me. He was a skinny kid who looked like a young Ron Wood. He could have worn Jade's jeans, his waist was so tiny. I always felt the need to fatten him up; I'd cook lavish meals for the whole band whenever they'd come over to the house. It was my motherly way of taking care of him. I suppose that's why Bret was so okay with our relationship. He trusted us completely and never complained about all the time we spent together, even when we stayed out all night. As long as I was with Marc, Bret was okay with it.

I also became close friends with Dan, their drummer. Whenever the two of us got together it was trouble. We were like gasoline and matches, especially when it came to drugs. Aside from the drugs, Dan, like Marc, was a really down-to-earth guy; they didn't have rock-star egos like so many other guys in bands. Sometimes they'd even mark out and tell their friends that they couldn't believe I was hanging out with them. They saw Bret wrestling in huge stadiums and wondered what I was doing with them in grubby little bars. I never thought about it like that though.

Whenever the band had a show in town, I'd drag Wanda or our nanny, Anna, out to see them. Bret would occasionally come along, and even joined them on stage once for a rendition of "Born to Be Wild," as he had done before with the original band, Steppenwolf. After their sets, we'd hang out and drink or head upstairs to do a few lines. Some nights the boys and I would grab some beers, go out to the hills that overlooked Calgary and talk into the night about our messed up lives. Marc was the only one of us who hadn't had a damaging childhood. His parents were as good as it gets. His dad was the head of a psychiatric hospital outside of Calgary, and his mother was as sweet as can be. Perhaps that upbringing was what made him such a wise and caring person. Time and time again, he would prove to be my anchor. Marc had a good head on his shoulders, but he wasn't without his rock oddities. He would write songs while sitting in an empty bathtub with his guitar, in the dark.

Some nights Bret would babysit Blade while I stayed out until the sun came up. He'd be eating breakfast when I came in, and would casually ask me how my night was and if I needed a Halcion. I guess he knew what I had been up to. I always felt like shit and terribly guilty, but Bret never made me feel like I was doing anything wrong. I suppose, like me, he had his own little secrets.

Marc became a permanent fixture in our home and eventually moved right in. Bret loved having him around. He introduced Bret to all kinds of new music. When I first met Bret, his taste in music was more sensitive than you might expect from a wrestler. He was always listening to really sad, mellow songs. I couldn't help but chuckle when he talked about his love of the Bee Gees—it just didn't fit with his tough image. Marc knew all about the new sounds coming out of Seattle, grunge bands like Mother Love Bone and Green River, and he got Bret into them as well. Bret particularly liked "Chloe," a Mother Love Bone song Marc had played for him.

Marc also got along great with the kids, especially the boys. Blade would tease Marc incessantly, while Dallas found quiet inspiration in Marc's guitar. Dallas eventually took up the drums because of Marc, though he was more interested in Green Day and dying his hair green than in Marc's music. Having Marc around made Dallas feel like it wasn't so odd to be different. He'd see Marc sitting on the couch in his Doc Martens, watching The Simpsons with a flannel shirt wrapped around his head like a towel, and think it was the coolest. Marc never got annoyed with the kids for anything, even when they came charging into his bedroom bright and early, the morning after a gig. When Blade would jump on his waterbed to wake him up, he'd just leap up and playfully chase after him.

Family life suited Marc, but he didn't leave his old lifestyle behind. He brought it with him. Our house turned into a hotel, full of musicians and their friends. We'd throw huge pool parties—though I'd often spend them tucked away in the sauna with Dan doing lines. Bret never said anything about it, though he had to have known what was happening. I was surprised he never questioned me about it. After all, Dan was gorgeous, with his waist-long hair, and had a charming personality. It sometimes made me wonder if he even cared.

I eventually found out that Michelle had been seeing Marc on the sly. Nobody knew—they had been careful about keeping it a secret. Apparently, she'd sometimes stick around after the rest of us had gone to bed, stay with Marc and then take off before we woke up. Michelle's marriage to Tom had been falling apart for a long time. A serious back injury and drug addiction had taken their toll on Tom, his career and his family. Months of uncertainty, idle threats and shouting matches culminated in Michelle's decision to leave him for good. She'd had enough of his bad temper and flights of rage, and sent him on a one-way trip back to England. Marc moved into Michelle's place and became a surrogate father to her children, especially Amaris, who is like a daughter to him to this day.

That August, my brother Mark committed suicide. Michelle and I were completely devastated. I can't even imagine how Michelle would have handled it without the love and support of Marc. I fell into despair and isolated myself from all of my friends. I blamed my parents and hated them for what happened to Mark. Nothing made sense anymore. I suffered in silence and found solace in the mickies of Jack Daniels I stashed under various sinks throughout the house.

Things were looking up for Bret and his career, though they were about to take a turn for the worse. I remember him calling home one night after being out with the boys and Vince McMahon in San Antonio. He told me excitedly that they had been drinking and goofing around—and that they had pulled the Hart Foundation's signature move on Vince. My reaction wasn't as gleeful as Bret's. I was worried for him, worried about what Vince might do to get him back. I told him that Vince would never forget it. Bret assured me that they were just treating Vince like one of the boys, and that there would be no retaliation. I said I wouldn't be so sure. It turned into a bit of an argument, with Bret not sounding as certain as he claimed to be. My parting words were, "Someday Vince will remember the Alamo…" I knew Bret could patch things up for a while, but I also believed that one day those words would ring true.

So maybe after all of those years Vince did remember the Alamo. Maybe that's what set the stage for the infamous Montreal Screwjob. Bret had signed a twenty-year contract with the WWF in 1996. A year later, while Bret was in his fifth reign as WWF Champion, Vince decided he wanted out of the deal and suggested Bret negotiate with WCW, the WWF's main competitor. Bret was scheduled to fight his last match with the WWF in Montreal, where he was regarded as a national hero. He was looking forward to winning in Canada and going out with glory before heading to WCW.

The day of the match was an extremely emotional one for Bret and our family. He felt very loyal to Vince and was reluctant to leave the WWF. The tension between Bret and Vince had been building leading up to Montreal, and Bret was vaguely worried about how it might affect the show, though he never expected it to end the way it did. We arrived in Montreal early that Sunday, and there were already hints of trouble that seem alarming in retrospect. Someone told Bret that morning that they had seen his opponent, Shawn Michaels, and Vince at the same hotel, getting into an elevator together, the night before.

It was also a day of sad goodbyes for everyone. The kids, Michelle and I spent a few hours backstage saying goodbye to the WWF crew and talent, some of whom were like family to us. A few moments were captured for *Wrestling with Shadows*, a documentary about Bret's life: I was there with everyone from WWF Diva Tammy Lynn Sytch, aka Sunny, to the referee of that night's main event, Earl Hebner, when I said, "My kids have all grown up with them…all of them. It's kinda funny hugging everyone and saying 'take care,' 'stay in touch'…you know they mean well. Some of them will keep in touch, but they'll never see any of these guys again, they'll just be a memory."

I was sitting with our lawyer, chatting and watching Bret's big match, when about fifteen minutes into the match the bell rang unexpectedly, over and over again. Bret was on the floor, in a hold, but he hadn't submitted. "Holy shit, that's not supposed to happen!" I exclaimed. "No, it's not," our lawyer said, equally astonished at what had just transpired in the ring.

Within seconds, Shawn had the belt and was being rapidly escorted backstage with Triple H. Bret spat on Vince from the ring as security guards emerged and came towards them. Owen and Davey Boy were in the ring standing beside Bret, who looked shocked beyond words.

Our lawyer and I jumped over the arena's hockey boards and ran backstage, trailing Bret and Blade, who were being escorted by security guards. It was pure chaos: Bret was walking at top speed down the hallway to the dressing room and was in such a zone. I tried to talk to him, but he just kept marching towards the dressing room. Everyone else started going in: The Undertaker, Triple H, Vince, Davey, and Owen. The door was shut, and the *Wrestling with Shadows* crew was asked to leave. We were all standing around waiting, listening to the noises inside the dressing room get louder and louder, though we were unable to discern what was being said. I sent the kids off with Bret's assistant.

I saw Triple H standing outside the room and snapped at him. I dressed him up and down and yelled that he was in on it, and that God would strike him down. I was so furious that the words just came out of me. These were people whom we considered friends and role models to our kids, and some of them double-crossed us at the very end.

Bret debuted with WCW to a lot of hype in December, appearing first on Monday Nitro, and then at their big pay-per-view event, Starrcade. He didn't actually wrestle until two months later, however, because he'd broken his hand in his fight with Vince.

With Montreal still a fresh wound, the holidays were anything but merry as 1997 drew to a close. To me, the incident was just another trial for our struggling family. I had no idea what was going on with Bret and me, my health was bad, and I was boozing a lot and doing cocaine from time to time. I was sure I had some undiagnosed illness that my doctor couldn't see. A smothering sensation followed me constantly; I couldn't catch my breath and every day I woke up stiff and sore, like someone had physically beaten me.

I felt ill, anxious, and driven to write in my journal, but with Bret being home and expecting perfect order, I knew it would be impossible. I suggested the possibility of hiring the housekeeper as a nanny, even though I knew it would create conflict and probably be out of the question. I tried explaining that I wasn't shirking my responsibilities and that I just needed some space, but he still refused. I felt that Bret was being too controlling, as usual, and let him know it, and he justified it by saying I was too impulsive and irrational. Bret ended the argument by saying maybe we were both sick of doing what we were doing, because he was sick of his routine too. He left to fly out to another show and I didn't kiss him or say goodbye. I just felt so disappointed and frustrated with him.

When he left I went downstairs to Bret's assistant Caroline's office to distract myself. We had both been reading *The Celestine Prophecy* and loved to chat about the book. We sat drinking tea and talking about our hopes for our lives. A couple of hours later Bret called from Salt Lake City to see if I had calmed down. I had, because he had gone. Bret said we had to get together with the kids when he got back to discuss our lives. I agreed and felt an anxious twinge in my stomach. I wondered what he had in mind. Feeling as though Bret had me on hold always brought me down. I had no idea about his other woman or their relationship at this point, but my intuition was telling me something. I was worried, but I also felt like I was at another crossroads in my life, and there was a new road in front of me I wouldn't mind following. Bret came home and informed me that he'd failed a test for steroids. It wasn't the first time. I felt that there had to be more on Bret's mind, but he didn't mention it.

We moved through the days as usual. I started to dread Bret coming home. I cringed when I would hear him coming up the stairs at night to come to bed. I avoided him more than ever and made excuses to be out of the house. He didn't seem to notice much either way. I wanted a break from everything, so I took

Jade to New York to celebrate her birthday. We had a great trip, but eerily spent a lot of time talking about divorce. One of her friends' parents had been going through it at the time. I wanted to calm her fears, so I told her not to worry—we would never put her and her siblings through that. I felt unsure of that as I spoke, but wanted to keep up the illusion of a happy home for my kids.

On our plane ride back to Calgary, I had that familiar feeling that something was wrong. Something was up with Bret. Sure enough, as soon as Jade and I got home, Bret asked to speak with me upstairs. I'll never forget the positions of our bodies. Bret was in a familiar pose, with his hands behind his head, as if to keep it from falling off. He appeared fully confident about what he was about to say. I was standing behind a chair when he very casually said, "I'm not going to mince words with you, Julie. I want a divorce." Just as casually, I replied, "Okay." I left him sitting there, ran down the stairs, jumped in my truck, and drove off. I wasn't sure where to, but my fight-or-flight instincts took over. I pulled into a parking lot and sat there dazed for a few minutes. It all suddenly hit me. I called Michelle and with anxiety in my voice said, "Michelle, Bret just asked me for a divorce." I felt lightheaded and wasn't really able to listen to her. She sounded so far away. Bret's words swirled around in my head, competing for attention. In between Michelle's expressions of concern for me and the occasional expletive, I heard nothing.

After the initial shock of the big "D" word, I checked into a hotel for a night. My pager kept going off, but I knew it was Bret and couldn't bear to talk to him, so I ignored it. I was numb and sat on the bed, listening to the hum of the air conditioner. I wished for the air conditioner to freeze me into further numbness and silence my thoughts. I sat on the floor, I sat in front of the mirror, I sat on the chair, but no matter where I sat, there I was. Sleep didn't come easily; I was so restless I felt like my head was going to pop off my shoulders. There is no use trying to rationalize things or calm yourself down when you're in that kind of emotional pain, reeling at the frightening possibility that your competition's waist is a size four and she laughs at everything he says.

The next morning I went to see my therapist, Irene. I didn't want to be in this position of helplessness and hopelessness. I had felt abused and ashamed for so many months, but my abandonment issues were keeping me from embracing my freedom. Irene spoke of boundaries, and picking myself up, but I was too overcome with anger to listen. It was easier and more comfortable for me to blame others than accept that I had a hand in the collapse of our marriage. I thought of my parents and resented them for fucking up my childhood and damaging my ability to have a stable relationship. Pick myself up? How was I supposed to do that on my own, with four kids to raise? I left with little comfort or hope and drove back home.

The kids were happy to see me, but confused by my distance. I walked upstairs and started taking things out of my closet. I was throwing them into a big pile when Jade came into the room and asked where I was going. I told her, "Your dad wants a divorce. I'm leaving—I will not stay in the same house as him." I was so lost in my anger I didn't even think of the damage I was doing. I finished packing without knowing where I was going. I thought of Michelle's, but was worried we'd just spend our time bashing Bret and Tom, instead of helping each other. I decided the best thing to do would be to find another hotel; at least there I could mourn and cry in private, without worrying about affecting the kids.

I got to the hotel and started to write in my journal. I wrote with passion and a fiery desire to exorcize my feelings. On the page my emotions were terribly confused: I cursed Bret and begged him to come home and forget everything. One minute I was loving towards him, and the next I was feeling deeply betrayed. My penmanship changed wildly, from neat to illegible and back. Bret continued to page me the entire time, but I wanted to try and resolve my feelings in writing first. Nothing was really accomplished; I didn't gain any emotional clarity and still felt devastated.

I soon found out why Bret had been paging me like crazy. Paul, the director of *Wrestling with Shadows*, was back in Calgary and needed us to reshoot an important scene. I spoke with Paul and explained our situation, saying there was no way I was doing anything to help Bret. He was surprisingly sympathetic. I had only told a few of our mutual friends about the divorce so far, and had been hurt by their insensitivity. For the most part, all I got from anyone close to Bret was, "Get over it, shit happens." I had suspected this would happen, but still felt abandoned by many people I once considered friends. I knew that some of them were two-faced and valued a relationship with Bret more than with me. I no longer served a purpose for them; it was only important to have Bret as a friend. Bret deserved these friends more anyway—he also never gave without expecting something in return. It was almost a matter of principle for Bret. I saw it in his relationships and heard it in his version of what friendship meant.

I ended up agreeing to reshoot the scene as a favour to Paul. I arrived at the house, and after Paul went over what we needed to do, we started filming. It was extremely surreal to talk to Bret as though nothing had happened. After we shot the scene Bret asked me to come upstairs to talk for a minute. I reluctantly followed him up the stairs, thinking now what? I sat on the bed, and he shut the door and stood in front of me. I looked away and asked him what he wanted. All he said was, "You know what I want." He took my hand, pulled me up, and led me to the bathroom. I don't know why I didn't resist. I guess in the back of my mind I hoped he was coming to his senses and would ask me to stay with him. "One for the road," he said afterwards. I left ashamed, feeling stupid that I had given in to his charms. I didn't mention it to any of my friends; I didn't want them to know how weak I was.

The next time Bret spoke to me he told me to get a lawyer, because he had already seen one. I knew Bret must have hired the best, but wasn't that worried about it. I spoke with Caroline about finding a reasonable fellow who didn't cost a fortune, but she advised me to get a tough one. I would later find out why, but at the time I was a little taken aback. I wasn't expecting a nasty fight, and I didn't think I would need someone who would go for the throat. I felt that if I were too hard on Bret, I would lose all hope of him ever coming back.

Anyway, I preferred to do my own fighting. For the next month it felt like I was spending most of my time fighting on the phone with Bret. For someone who wanted to end it, he sure called a lot, if only to call me a whore. He yelled that he hadn't worked so hard and taken all those bumps over the years just to have me take all of his money. I would occasionally try to raise my voice a decibel over his to challenge his self-centredness and remind him that raising four children is hard work. Bret wouldn't hear of it and we usually just hung up on each other. The conversations were so passive aggressive and emotionally draining that sometimes I felt like he was just trying to wear me out. There were moments when he spoke to me in softness, but it was usually just because he wanted something. It was only after years of marriage that I was able to see through his deceptions, which were spun of the finest gold. I suppose that's why he thought of himself as the best in the business; his ability to deceive was so total, it carried into his personal life.

One day I got a call from a friend asking me what was happening with the child support. "He's being unreasonable. He figures since I have the house and the car, I should go easy on the child support. We're still negotiating." She was very quiet, so I asked her what was wrong.

"Just don't sign anything, promise?"

"Okay, but why?"

"You need to talk to Caroline."

"Why?" I asked, though I didn't really want to know.

"Do not sign those fucking papers, Julie. It will be the stupidest move you will ever make. Call Caroline. She will tell you why."

I put the phone down and stared at it. I knew even before calling what she was going to tell me. I hesitated and then grabbed the phone angrily, as though the phone was at fault for revealing my darkest fears.

Caroline's mom answered and said she wasn't there. I hung up, a little relieved that I wouldn't have to hear anything. That didn't last long, though; my gloomy curiosity soon got the best of me. I tried again, but she still wasn't there. I paced back and forth, wondering if she was going to tell me that she and Bret were having an affair. I often caught Caroline looking at me with pity and wondered why. I called her again. Her mom, whom I had clearly irritated, dropped the phone and called her name.

"Hello?" Her voice sounded so sad and weak, almost like a whisper.

"Caroline, it's Julie. Caroline, what's wrong? I was told to call you before I signed my child support papers."

"Julie, I don't know what to say to you. I'm such a coward and I feel so bad."

"Caroline, is it Bret? You aren't…"

"Oh my God, no, not me. There's someone else, Julie, and they have been together for a while."

I suppose it shouldn't have shocked me or caused the air to be sucked from my lungs, but it did. I asked questions and made myself listen to all of the answers. All these months Caroline had been arranging their get-togethers. Her name was Christine, and Caroline would book her tickets to fly and meet Bret whenever he was in the States. Caroline said she had been wanting to quit because she so hated having to deceive me. I heard about a lot more that night, and when I hung up, I was going to war.

Hell hath no fury like a woman sucker punched. I was livid. I banged and kicked things and stared at the phone, daring it to ring. I wanted Bret to call so I could make him feel some of the pain that was tearing me in two. When he did call, I was surprisingly controlled. I felt that years of deceit and manipulation deserved an ominous response and simply said, "Caroline told me everything and you are fucked." After a moment's stunned silence, I added, "I'm not signing those papers!" Feeling empowered, I hung up the phone. I called my lawyer and informed him I wouldn't be signing the papers yet, as there were new developments and I needed time to think. I took the phone off the hook again, partly because I needed to get my thoughts together, and also because I knew it would drive Bret nuts. I had very mixed emotions; I wanted to fight, but I also wanted to curl up in self-pity over the betrayal. Most of all I felt manipulated. He had been pressuring me to sign the papers because he was afraid that if I found out about the girlfriend, I would take him to the cleaners.

After a few hours I put the phone back on the hook and it immediately rang. Bret denied everything and claimed that Caroline had made everything up because she was jealous. When that didn't work, he tried to blame me, saying that I was no longer the person he fell in love with. The verbal abuse from both of us escalated until I couldn't take any more and hung up. I sat dazed and cried heavily. The crying came from deep in my chest, and was unlike anything I had ever experienced before. It frightened me because it made me feel so weak. I wasn't just mourning my relationship, I was stirring up all of the negative energy that I had been repressing for years.

Eventually Bret came out with the whole truth and told me about Christine. He told me more than I ever asked to know or needed to know. He sat in my house and informed me that she wasn't built like a stripper and she made him laugh. And she was ten years younger than me. And she loved kids, and he was sure she'd love ours. I sat there shaking my head, wondering if he was fucking insane. He also gave me his reasons for wanting to leave me. Apparently he was haunted by what happened to me as a kid and couldn't take it anymore. Also, I was getting heavier and wasn't taking care of myself anymore. It was all such bullshit. He even told me that he wished me the best. Ah yes, the best there is, the best there was, the best there ever will be.

It was important for me to keep my feet moving, but I felt like I was standing in quicksand. The couch started to look really good again. I spent the next three days lying around, staring at the walls. I wasn't aware of anything other than paying the pizza bill and occasionally seeing my face in the mirror when I went to the bathroom. I felt old at thirty and wondered how my life had turned out like this. I thought I had done everything I was supposed to. I had loved unconditionally, but had failed my marriage and failed to keep my kids from a broken home.

I was left alone to imagine Bret running on the beach in a thong, happily building sandcastles. It was a ridiculous image, but it made me laugh and prevented me from thinking about his actual new life. I went back and forth between thoughts of cruelty and thoughts of dread, of what I was going to miss about him. I was on my third day of woe when the doorbell rang. Surely it couldn't be the pizza man? It turned out God was sending an angel, in the form of Ashid Bahl. I opened the door and Ashid greeted me with a smile, saying he had just wanted to drop by to say hi. I was delighted, but surprised; I normally only saw him when Bret and I were doing charity work with his organization, the For the Love of Children Society of Alberta. Holding on to the door for support, I blurted out, "Ashid, Bret wants a divorce, and my life sucks and I can't even get off the couch."

"What? What happened?"

I let him in and he grabbed my hand kindly. "You need to pull yourself together in front of the kids. They shouldn't see you this way, Julie. They need you to be strong."

I explained what had happened, and he suggested I do some charity work to focus on something other than my problems with Bret. I had my doubts, wondering how I could help anyone else when I couldn't even help myself. I was also afraid of putting myself out there. I just wanted to hide until the divorce was over. Sometimes it felt like everyone's eyes and whispers were walking alongside me like a shadow. I didn't want to answer any boring, nosy questions about what went wrong between Bret and me. I didn't want people to see how much of slob Bret Hart's soon-to-be ex-wife had become. I was starting to wish I hadn't opened the door, when Ashid mentioned he was going to be opening a yoga school in Calgary and could use some help. The idea really appealed to me, and I told him I would give it some thought. I was at my worst, and the opportunity to take my mind off Bret, and help others find some peace of mind in the process, seemed like a gift from God.

Bret was still on the road a lot and stayed with our friend Dean whenever he slithered into Calgary. He would sometimes be home and not bother to call the kids. I would find out from friends that he was home and be furious with him. The kids would count down the days until he returned, and he would leave them counting. They had been expecting him to be home by Canada Day, and were hoping that he would take them out to see the fireworks. He called them on Canada Day, though he had been home for days, and told them that he was coming to pick them up. The kids stood on the street in front of the house, on and off, all afternoon waiting for him. Beans would come in with tears in her eyes, asking where he was. I angrily called his cell, which he had shut off. I totally lost my cool and called the kids inside to speak with them. I complained about their father and told them that he had a girlfriend whom he was probably busy smoking pot with. The older kids, Dallas and Jade, already knew about the pot; they had caught him reeking of it before. The girlfriend was news, and I told them exactly what I thought of her. I knew I had made a mistake when I saw how big and tear-filled Jade's eyes became. I had tarnished her image of her dad.

It was about nine o'clock in the evening when he finally showed up with Dean. They were both stoned and had been drinking. We were pulling out of the driveway as he pulled in; I was taking the kids to see the fireworks myself. I wanted to keep going, but he shouted at me. I told him I had talked to the kids about his recent behaviour. Then it was like everything happened in slow motion. Bret asked me to get out of the car, he wanted to talk to me alone. I told him to fuck off, and he punched at my window. That's when the kids really started to cry. I got out of the car, and he grabbed me by my jacket and led me away from the kids. He pulled me around to the side of the house and asked me what I had told them. I told him that they knew everything about his girlfriend, and had always known about the pot. He slammed me against the wall and said, "You fucking bitch, I hate you, I hate you!"

In my head I heard Bret saying something he had told me years ago: If you're ever in a fight, don't forget, the head always follows the body. So I saw what he was going to do next—because, in a way, he told me—but was still helpless to stop it. He grabbed me around the neck and slammed me on the ground. It knocked the wind out of me, and he continued to choke me, making sure I couldn't catch my breath. His knees were on my shoulders; I tried to pull him off with my legs, but couldn't get them high enough. Out of the corner of my eye I saw Blade running towards us, screaming for Bret to get off me. "Dad, leave her alone, get off!" Blade grabbed Bret's arms and tried to pull him off me. Suddenly, Bret let me go. I started coughing and gasping for air, and Bret grabbed Blade and took off. Dean came around the corner, "Holy shit, what's the matter with that guy?" I was in shock. My legs were shaking so badly I could barely stand up. Dean helped me into the house and I sat at the kitchen table, stunned. I asked where Blade was and Jade told me he had left with Bret. After what had just happened I was worried Blade might be in some kind of danger. I had never seen Bret so unstable and filled with hate. I picked up the phone and dialed 911. I anxiously recounted everything that had happened. I told the operator my husband tried to choke me to death and took our son.

"What's his name?"

"He's a wrestler," I said nervously.

"Which wrestler?"

"Bret 'Hitman' Hart. We're separated and I don't know where my son is."

The operator said he would send a car right away. I hung up the phone, already regretting the call. I worried about the papers getting hold of the story. The police arrived within minutes and saw the red marks on my neck and my crazily coifed hairstyle, courtesy of Bret Hart. They asked me if I wanted to press charges. I hadn't even thought of that—I just wanted Blade home. They encouraged me to file a report, but I said no. I didn't want to ruin Bret's career. The officers really didn't care who Bret was. They'd seen the signs of abuse and were disappointed that I wasn't going to do anything about it. They reminded me that I had a few days to come down to the station and file a report. I thanked them, and we set to tracking down Blade. I gave them Bret's cell number and they called until he picked up. The officer calmly told Bret to bring Blade home, his mom was worried about him. I interjected, saying that I didn't want Bret coming back here. The officer told Bret to take Blade to the police station, so that he could be picked up from there. I showed the policemen to the door, thanking them again. I still wonder what they were thinking as they pulled away from the house.

I called Michelle and told her what happened. She was astounded by Bret's behaviour—he had never done anything quite like this before. She said she would come with me to pick up Blade. We rode in silence to the station, and when we got there she ran in to get Blade. She came back alone. Apparently Blade had decided to stay with Bret for the night. I suddenly felt bad for us all.

I went home and sat outside on a swing by myself, reflecting on this disastrous Canada Day. Fireworks were nothing compared to the explosive anger on my lawn a few short hours ago. How had we ever come to this as a family? I cried for us all that night as I swung back and forth, trying to calm myself. I kept hearing Bret saying "I hate you" over and over, like a mantra in my head. The worst part was that we had put the kids through all of this. Bret and I had promised, from the very beginning, to never let the kids see us fighting. Our childhood homes had been filled with such dysfunction that we swore we would not allow history to repeat itself. And now, what had we done? Our children had witnessed terrible abuse, and they would never look at us as a source of safety and stability again.

I dragged myself upstairs and went to bed feeling restless. Bret had been planning to take the kids to Hawaii for a vacation, but now I wasn't sure I wanted them to go. I was worried he wouldn't bring them back. I eventually fell into an uneasy sleep, awaking in the morning to a pounding at the door. I froze. One of the kids let Bret in. He came up to my room and sat on my bed. I wanted to leave, but the aches and pains in my back and chest stopped me from going anywhere. I turned so I wouldn't have to face him. He started brushing my hair with his hands and apologizing for what had happened. I started crying, the tears stinging my face, which was raw from all the sobbing. I asked him not to touch me. He said that he hadn't meant to hurt me, but that I had hurt him by telling the kids about the pot and the girl. He begged me to let him take the kids to Hawaii;

after all, it was for his birthday, and I knew how he felt about his birthdays. For some reason I agreed.

I asked him where Blade was, and he said he had left him at Dean's to sleep. He casually asked if I would have a coffee with him downstairs. I couldn't believe the question and asked if he was serious. "Bret, are you aware of what we have become to one other? I am not sorry for what I said. I am only sorry that I hurt the children so badly. Blade will never forget this and he will be scarred for the rest of his life—all because we couldn't act like fucking adults." He didn't reply and just hung his head. I knew he was feeling ashamed. Later that day, I drove Bret and the kids to the airport, crying the entire time with Blade on my lap, his little hands wiping my tears.

When I got home I called Dean and asked if he wanted to go to Jamaica. I needed some peace and quiet, away from lawyers and phones and the past. I wanted Dean to come because I knew he would keep me from dwelling on the divorce. It was the quiet moments alone that I feared. I waited until the kids got back safe from Hawaii, looking like golden little nuts, and then set off. Our trip got off to a bad start: The plane's landing gear wouldn't go down, and we had to circle the airport several times. Dean was beside himself, anxiously grumbling that this would be a shitty way to die. I found myself unconcerned. I guess I had been through so much, I hardly believed it could get worse. As we circled around, I thought of how lucky it would be for Bret if we crashed and he didn't have to pay a dime. I could see his smirk upon hearing the news that my plane had crashed down out of the Florida skies. When we finally landed everyone cheered, but I was almost disappointed that we hadn't become some tragic headline.

When we got outside the humidity instantly hit us, as the familiar smell of island flowers wafted towards our chilled noses. It didn't take long before we encountered another familiar smell: A young Jamaican boy slid some weed into my hand and asked us if we wanted to buy any. Though we wanted some, we certainly weren't going to buy it from a kid. I handed it back to him, and Dean and I headed to the resort. The hotel was beautiful. I thought that from that point on everything was going to be alright. We took our bags to our room and ventured out for a walk. We headed to the beach in search of some good old Jamaican pot. There was an abundance of it everywhere. We laughed when we saw the size of the bag we had purchased. It was bursting at the seams—there was no way we'd be able to smoke it all. We took it back to our room and rolled some joints for the beach, then grabbed some tropical drinks and headed out to watch the sunset. I laughed harder than I had in a long time and was grateful that Dean was with me. We staggered back to the room laughing and passed out. I got up in the morning, sat on the deck with a coffee, and wondered what it would be like to move here and never have to hear Bret's name again.

We spent all of the next day on the beach. It was refreshing to wear a bikini and not give a shit who saw me. I was so sick of wearing oversized clothes to hide my body from Bret's scrutiny. It actually felt good to lie on the hot beach, spreading out like an egg in a frying pan. I watched Dean try to learn how to swim in three feet of water; he was terrified of being in water above his waist. I laughed at him from the beach, and whenever he came out of the water because the lifeguard was on break. I only went inside briefly to call the kids and see how they were doing. I picked up the phone with apprehension, fearing doom and gloom. Michelle answered and immediately told me that Bret had been calling relentlessly and questioning her about what I was doing in Jamaica. He had been demanding to know what I was doing, why I went with Dean, and if we were staying in separate rooms. I brushed off his concerns and told Michelle to ignore him. Let him have all the same dark, jealous thoughts I had over the years.

At night we went to a party full of people dancing and having a good time. Dean and I strolled around the many tables of food and heaped our plates high, unable to resist the tempting smells of the island dishes. There were little booths laid out with trinkets, and fortune tellers who sat patiently, waiting to deliver someone a glimmer of hope. I was drawn to one lady with silver bracelets that looked too heavy for her small arms. She didn't really tell me much about my past or future, which was kind of a relief. I just wanted to have fun at the party and stay in the moment.

I got back to the room feeling tired and happy. I was lying in bed as Dean flipped through TV channels. My heart dropped—there on the screen, like a cruel fucking joke, was Bret wrestling. I was as far away from him as I could get, and yet, there he was. I snapped at Dean to turn it off. It took me a long time to fall asleep that night, my head full of visions of Bret and his new laughing Barbie.

As soon as I got home the phone calls started again. Bret would complain that everyone was out to get him, especially me. He called me a money-hungry whore who was trying to ruin his life. He even got angry at me for things he imagined I would do in the future, saying I would probably try to ruin all of his relationships with women. I told him I'd be fine with him lying to someone else for change. My dismissiveness infuriated him; he wanted to believe that I would hunt down and seek revenge on any new girl. I started to tell him he needed to accept responsibility for the way his life was going and stop blaming others, but he cut me off, saying, "If I ever see Caroline again, I will hold her down with one foot and blow her fucking head off." I begged him to stop calling me. I wanted to gain control of my life and move on, but our calls kept setting me back and throwing me into emotional turmoil. He complied, but also stopped calling the kids, probably to punish me for my request. It took all my strength not to call him and bitch him out for it, but I didn't because I knew that was exactly what he wanted. His life had so much chaos in it and he thrived by projecting it onto me.

In person I could tell that all of Bret's anger was coming from a deep unhappiness. I could see it in his body language and the way he wore his hat pulled down tight around his eyes. I heard it in his voice when he gave TV interviews. It was as if he had "lost his smile," as Shawn Michaels once famously quipped. He seemed like he was running down a dream.

I also thought that the stress of the divorce was beginning to manifest itself physically, in both of us. Whenever I got extremely upset, my hands and feet would itch like crazy. Some days, I could barely walk because it felt like I was stepping on marbles. I saw my family doctor about it, and he assured me that it was being caused by stress. He told me it was nothing to worry about and recommended I find an emotional outlet for my anxiety. I heard from the kids that Bret was having the same problem. I thought it was so strange that Bret and I were experiencing the same symptoms, but assumed it was just a reaction to our mutual misery.

I set about making some changes in my life, starting with my home. Looking around, it occurred to me that Bret had chosen almost all of the furniture. I wanted everything that reminded me of him out. I got rid of all his cold, gloomy furniture and created the warm, welcoming home I had always wanted. I filled the house with comfortable furniture, earthy tones, and pottery the children had lovingly made with their chubby little fingers in kindergarten. I dug out paintings and drawings the kids had made for us over the years and proudly displayed them, replacing the death and gore of the art Bret had chosen. I was especially happy to take down a civil war print called "Give Them Cold Steel," which Bret was particularly fond of.

I did whatever I could to bring stability to our family. I tried to find things for us to focus on instead of the divorce. I continued helping Ashid with his yoga school and got the kids involved in a bunch of activities. The boys seemed most affected by their father's absence, and it showed in their attitudes towards school and extracurricular activities. I remember picking up Blade and Beans from their art class after a nasty fight with Bret, only to have Blade declare that he wanted to quit. He complained that they were making him draw baby stuff and defiantly said that he was never going back. I was feeling impatient and said that we would talk about it later. He continued to press me, saying he also wanted to drop out of school and only play hockey, and that he wanted to move in with his dad. I lost my resolve and broke into tears. When we arrived home Blade jumped out of the car, and Beans just stayed sitting in the backseat. Then, in all her innocence, she quietly said, "Don't worry, Mom. Everything and everybody will be okay." I looked back at her in my rear-view mirror and cried even harder.

Dallas wasn't handling things any better. For the next few months I would be in and out of meetings with counsellors and teachers to talk about his behaviour in class and his lack of commitment to his education. I sat and listened to the long list of misconduct. The longer the counsellor spoke, the further away she sounded. I only took in parts of what she was saying: Dallas has a chip on his shoulder, is disrespectful, won't work in class, lies in class, is resentful of directions, gives dirty looks to teachers. I felt the need to defend Dallas and reminded her that our family was in crisis. I was also feeling personally defensive as a mother struggling to get her children under control without the proper support from their father. Feeling ashamed and frustrated, I sarcastically told the counsellor to send the same list of problems to Dallas's father, and stood up and left. I spoke with Dallas later about his problems at school. He said he just hated school. I asked him if he wanted to speak with a therapist, but he just rolled his eyes and told me he wasn't mental.

"What about your dad?" I asked.

Dallas answered quietly, "He doesn't call and he's never home."

Wrestling, of all things, seemed to help the boys cope best. It allowed them to express their emotions and imaginations, and gave them a connection to their father. We still had a wrestling ring in our pool room, which overlapped the shallow end of the pool. The boys and their friends would come up with tag-team names and hold matches there. They would dream up elaborate storylines and promising futures for their characters. Jade would play Miss Elizabeth and accompany them into the ring. Bret continued to use the space as a training room and hired Leo Burke to train some of the new boys there. I felt that Blade and Dallas needed male influences in their lives, so I kept the stupid wrestling school thing going even though it reminded me of everything I had lost.

With Bret at a distance and the kids busy, our lives began to stabilize. I, of course, sabotaged everything by starting to sleep with him again. He would pick me up and drive us somewhere dark and secretive, then drop me off in the same manner. I was amused by this behaviour until I stopped to think: how many others had he done this very same thing with? I started to feel upset by the callous disregard he had for me after our clandestine meetings, but knew it wasn't going to end, and that I'd be climbing right back into his truck.

Once, before we parted ways, I noticed his hunched shoulders and lowered head and bluntly asked, "Are you happy?"

"No, I can't get happy. Are you?"

"I'm trying to, but it will come."

"Are you seeing anyone? It doesn't matter, but I guess you probably are."

"No," I said, knowing exactly why he was asking. It was part of the game of seduction. I would feel sorry for him, and he would get what he needed in the moment and go home. I mistook codependence for love and stayed stuck in our toxic relationship.

I longed to find the strength to finally move on. I prayed for God to intervene and worked with my therapist on establishing boundaries, but in the end it was Bret who put a stop to things. He called to tell me that we needed to have a mutual understanding of where things stood, and that we couldn't keep doing what we were doing. I was perplexed, but not for long; I heard a door open over the phone and suddenly realized he was in the company of Christine. He continued his performance, trying to impress her by sounding in charge and loudly recounting a distorted version of our situation. He said things that fell completely out of the context of our conversation, just so that she would hear his heroic monologue. I calmly told him he was full of shit, and said, "I don't know what's going on with you right now, but you're making all those stories about deadbeat dads come true. So the next time you call me for a quick pickup, you should ask your girlfriend if she minds getting sloppy seconds." I hung up the phone, enraged and disappointed in myself for being so gullible just a few short days ago.

The next time Bret called it was with a warning. He told me he'd gotten a test for hepatitis after going to the doctor to find out why his hands wouldn't stop itching, and said I should probably get tested too. The fear of passing something so deadly onto my kids inspired a massive round of swearing and name-calling: "How dare you do this to them, expose them to your fucking behaviour. You fucking lowlife, I curse you and every girl you've ever been with for putting my children in danger because of your self-centredness." I don't think I even took a breath in that moment of fear and anger. I heard nothing but silence from his end. I started to cry uncontrollably and said, "You have violated me in so many ways, psychologically and physically, and I am pleading with you to stay away from me. Please, God, stay away from me." I hung up, but within moments we were back to cursing at each other. I tore him apart as though it was the last time we would speak to each other. I said, "You are a man without conscience, who will never know what it means to stand for something morally. I will never forgive you for the betrayals. In all your bullshit, you have justified yourself by saying that I have betrayed you. Your problem lies deeper than anything I have ever done or said to you. Your fucked-up way of escaping responsibility for all the girls you've been with, as though you had to do it—saying life on the road is hard, and thank God you didn't fall victim to drugs or alcohol. I would have accepted that more readily than the mouth of a woman wrapped so deliciously around your dick." I hung up the phone and kicked the table hard. I prayed he wouldn't call back.

I heard from the kids that Bret had taken Christine up to his parents' to show her the house and introduce her to everybody. The Hart boys always brought girls up there when they wanted to impress them. The tour started with the chandeliers, Persian rugs, and Chippendale furniture, and ended with the infamous Dungeon. I later heard from others in the Hart family about Christine's age — she was only a year older than Jade. I wanted to warn her that someday she would see through Bret's brilliantly painted facade. I wanted to tell her to read The Picture of Dorian Gray, so that she wouldn't be shocked by the loathsome character beneath Bret's image.

Bret took Blade and Beans to Las Vegas for Halloween Havoc. He ended up leaving them with a mutual friend for most of the time while he and Christine disappeared. Apparently they spent the whole time fighting; Christine wanted to hang around backstage during the show, near the curtain Bret made his entrance from, but one of the agents told her to take a seat and she threw a fit. If I had ever done that at a wrestling show, I wouldn't have been allowed back.

Blade was playing in his very first hockey game, which he had been excited about for weeks. He was so happy to finally get on the ice and compete. "I can't believe this," he said as he put on his jersey. "I'm finally a player." It was also my first sight of Bret in a while. We sat apart because I was still angry and couldn't stand to look at him. I focused on Blade as he glided across the ice. I was so proud of him. He kept looking over to see if we were watching him, and would cheer with us as he skated past. I had some things I needed to say to Bret, but I didn't want to get into an argument at the game, so I handed him a note. During the third period I went to get a coffee, and Bret, upset with my lack of communication, approached me.

"What the fuck is this?" he asked.

I cut to the chase. "I need you to kick in more money for Blade's hockey equipment and any other activities the kids do."

Bret shifted his attention back to the game, but as soon as the buzzer went he said, "You can go fuck yourself, you fucking whore. I'm not giving you another dime!" As it was with our patterns of behaviour, Bret called me two days later, wanting to have coffee. I had no idea what was up. I had been feeling bad about pecking his character to death and agreed to meet him at a nearby restaurant. It was a public place, which meant that, hopefully, there wouldn't be any screaming or fighting. We pulled up at the same time and both looked at what was a very small, not-very-private place to talk. Bret nervously suggested his house. I said no, but he pressed me. "Come on, you haven't even seen my house." I reluctantly agreed, and he jumped in my car. He took me on a tour of his new home, which looked like Ben Cartwright's ranch on *Bonanza*. I imagined him living in the sprawling bungalow all by himself, in relative seclusion from the peering eyes of the world. He took me to the back of the house, near his bedroom, and we sat on the ledge of the fireplace to drink our coffee. We were just chatting when he took my face in his hands and kissed me passionately on the lips. We had angry sex, as if we were using our bodies to express our pain. In between the heavy lovemaking, he told me he still loved me. I felt the pit of my stomach roll with a familiar crest of fear. I couldn't trust him, and I certainly couldn't believe what he said.

After a few hours, Bret said his personal coach was coming to train him, but I could stay if I wanted. I told him I had things to do.

"Well, you can come back if you want to. Maybe you could show me how to work the barbeque."

"Sure, when?" I answered, like any codependent would.

"I'll call you when I'm done."

I went home and waited, reflecting on what had happened, looking for hidden motives and manipulations. I felt uneasy and wondered about his relationship with his girlfriend. In my mind I replayed his voice telling me he loved me, analyzing it for authenticity. I wondered when his trainer would leave, or when the coast would be clear for me to return. I found myself stuck waiting by the phone, getting angrier and more anxious by the minute. Should I be happy? I couldn't tell. When he finally called I spoke with an air of fatalism, as though I expected him to say that what we had done had been a mistake. He didn't, and I went back to his house, arriving to the smell of another cup of coffee brewing and quietness from him. We spent the evening together, and I left still uncertain if I was being played.

After a few days without another phone call from Bret, I began to feel used again. I decided to refocus my energy on my charity work with Ashid. I attended meetings for the Society's upcoming Christmas charity event, a fundraiser and show for terminally ill children called Santa's Express. We planned to have the kids flown around Calgary on small planes, so that they could catch an aerial glimpse of Santa arriving in his helicopter. I felt good about how I was using my time and encouraged by my friends. I left the meetings feeling like I had extra air in my Nikes. At our final meeting before the event, Ashid informed us that he had asked Bret to be a part of it. One of my friends kicked my leg under the table and rolled her eyes. I was upset at first, and started to protest, but Ashid calmed me down. He said that they needed a celebrity, that the kids would enjoy it, and he was right. In the end, I didn't let it bring me down. I was just happy to be helping children. I felt like I had found something bigger than Bret Hart.

A few days before Santa's Express, Bret called to see if I was upset with him. In a very flat tone I asked, "What is it that you want?"

"I just wanted to know what you were doing for Christmas," he said, in a rather childlike voice.

Bret knew I'd be spending it at home with the kids, and I had heard that he was taking Christine up to the Hart house, so I just replied, "You know what I'm doing." I waited for him to speak. I heard him sigh and ask if coffee was possible. I replied, "You know, whenever we do coffee it ends up being something else." He assured me he just wanted to talk and asked if he could come over. He was being so vague, and I was getting sick of his games, so I told him I was busy and that I'd see him at the fundraiser.

It was a crisp winter morning and I was wide awake at seven o' clock, eager to see our plans come to life. After their plane rides, the kids were treated to a match between Bret Hart and Darth Vader, who was plotting to stop Santa Claus from coming to Calgary. I remember thinking it was too bad Ashid didn't give Darth a real lightsaber to slice the Hitman's head off his droopy shoulders. Anyway, the kids were delighted, and when it was done I went over to Bret to shake his hand and thank him for helping out. It was an awkward moment; people were looking at us, waiting for me to give my hero husband a big wet kiss.

A couple of weeks before the holidays Bret called to ask if he could stay over on Christmas Eve. I thought of all the Christmases he had missed while wrestling, and how I resented Vince and the WWF for taking him away from us so often. Bret mentioned how it was our first year without a Christmas card picture. He seemed truly melancholy, and I felt myself soften. I asked, without prying too much, about Christine. He said that he had ended it with her, that she was a psycho. I listened while staring at my fingernails, tapping them as he spoke. Part of me was gratified that he was feeling as confused and distraught as I had been.

> I sat nervously waiting for you to come for dinner. Jade commented on your arrival, saying it was as though you were a guest. I looked at her sadly and said,

"Maybe that's all he should be." It felt awkward having you over. I didn't know how the dinner would go or if it would be even harder for the kids. You asked if they had enough presents and I told you yes, so that you wouldn't be frightened or ashamed of not bearing any. I feared you wouldn't come. I waited for the opening of my front door, like I had for so many years. I'm thinking back to the conversation we had last night as we lay in bed together, and am biting my pen as I recall your moments of callousness. You shared stories about Christine that made me shiver with disgust that I had allowed you in my bed to speak of other women. I listened as you talked about other girls, and how I would be proud of you for having what you described as thoughtless blowjobs. I felt like stabbing you with the pain that stiffened my muscles like steel, while I lay beside you and listened to you describe true love, which was what we had. I let you rattle on about your favourite writers, like Mark Helprin, and how you felt like one of the characters in his book, A Soldier of the Great War. At some point I found my senses disassociating from your stories. I became numb and restless and said it was time to sleep. You have been to hell and back again, I thought silently. I rolled over to face the wall as I had done for so many years, when you were still mine.

I wrote that as I waited for Bret on Christmas Eve. He had stayed over the night before as well. I had let him back into my arms for the holidays.

A new year was upon us, and I felt like a change was coming. I wrote my resolutions for 1999. The first one was not to sleep with the enemy, a headstrong resolution which would soon be subject to revision. Bret came over for dinner on New Year's Day. We shared our favourite songs of the year and our resolutions, as we had every year. One of my resolutions was for Bret and me to build a solid foundation of friendship, before we even considered getting back together. Bret told me his top resolutions, which included continuing to love his family and making peace with his demons. His last resolution gave me pause: figure out my future down the road. It was an ambiguous statement. He could have been talking about his career, but I couldn't help but wonder if he meant his future with me. We had been rebuilding our relationship, but this seemed to reveal his uncertainty about us. To make things worse, he was headed out on the road again. We were back to our late-night calls. It actually felt safer to reveal our feelings with the miles between us. We talked about our fears and hopes, though we both kept our guard up when talking about the future. At the time I was just glad he had come back to me, even if we were living in separate homes.

Regardless of what was happening with Bret and me, I tried to keeping living the best life I could. I offered to host the Society's annual appreciation dinner at my house. The date was approaching, and I was running around trying to organize the party and get the house ready. Bret gave me back his *Lonesome Dove* portrait, which had been taken while he was guest starring on the show. I hung it alongside our newer family pictures. It was the most handsome picture of Bret I had ever seen. I didn't want Bret to feel like he had been wiped out of existence.

The house was in perfect order, and as I waited for the caterer to arrive, I couldn't help but think that everything felt magical. The only setbacks were those little moments of anxiety that whispered cautions in my head—don't get ahead of yourself. As I walked around the house and had a last look to see if the kids had made a mess, I thought of the many parties we hadn't had because Bret was too preoccupied or wanted quiet when he came home from the road. I stood in front of the mirror in my bedroom and told myself that I was on my way. I looked at the outfit I had picked for the evening and saw that, for the first time in a long time, I looked elegant and sophisticated. It was quite a change from the frumpy, baggy clothes of the past few years. I looked at my eyes in the mirror and saw a glimpse of happiness. I was brought back to the moment by the sound of the doorbell: my guests had arrived.

I mingled and floated around as my friends and the various volunteers walked around the house and admired the way I had decorated it. The compliments I cherished most were about my children. I had pictures of them everywhere, and their art displayed on every shelf in the house. Bret's portrait became a conversation piece. Most of my guests were aware of our situation, and that we were trying to work things out, but no one really knew where things stood. How strange it was to have them ask about him. How uncomfortable it was to have to explain that he no longer lived here. I felt that twinge of shame again, of failure, which occasionally surfaced in moments like these and convinced me I wasn't going to make it.

Ashid toasted everyone who had contributed to making the year a success and gave little speeches about each volunteer. Everyone in turn thanked Ashid for all his selfless work. As I said goodbye to everyone at the end of the night, and shut the door behind the last guest, I knew for certain that I was coming into my own.

I was cleaning the dishes when Bret called. He said he had been listening to his tapes—he always kept an audio diary when he was on the road—and doing a lot of thinking. I interrupted with an "Uh-oh," and he went on to say he had been looking at himself a lot lately and needed to see me to talk.

When he returned, the talk we had was full of passion, as if it had never escaped us. During the quiet gaps in our conversation,

I held him tight. I wanted to stay quiet so that the spell wouldn't be broken. It was strange how easily I became mute when trying to tell Bret my true feelings, and sad how I only spoke the truth in anger. .

Bret and I went on vacation to Hawaii so I could read the manuscript for the autobiography he was writing (*Hitman: My Real Life in the Cartoon World of Wrestling*), and we could work on our relationship. I knew I had to tell him the truth about how I felt, about my hopes that we would get back together. When I did, he brazenly replied, "I don't live by anyone's rules, and I don't want to be rushed into another trap." I was hurt by that remark, and by what was being revealed to me through the manuscript, and snapped back, "That's it, I can't do this anymore! I want to stop playing this game and move on!" He agreed, and we both got up and started to walk to the hotel. Out of the blue, as though he wanted to say it while he still had the chance, he said, "My therapist said sometimes girls, like the age you were when all that stuff happened to you, like it." I stopped dead in my tracks and kicked him as hard as I could, right in the middle of the street. I was devastated and burst into tears. I quickly walked away, determined that this was the last time he would ever make me feel ashamed. He tried grabbing my arm to slow me down, but I wrestled free of his grip and broke into a faster pace. I was already packing my bag when he came into the room, demanding to know where I was going. When I wouldn't answer him, he grabbed my bag and threw it against the wall. "If you go, don't ever come back." After another disastrous fight, I left Hawaii completely hopeless. I later found out he'd only invited me because two other women had cancelled on him.

Before the nineties were through, the Hart's would face another family tragedy. Blade, Dallas and I had just returned from a Calgary Hitmen game in Ottawa when Michelle called with the news: "Julie, something happened to Owen. I don't know what's going on." No one could get a hold of Bret, he was on a plane to California. I called Stu. I could tell it was bad because I could hear Helen crying in the background. Michelle came over and we drove right to the Hart house. Alison was hysterical, as was Helen. Vince called to confirm the Harts' worst nightmare. Owen had been wrestling in a paper-per-view event in Kansas City, and while attempting to make a dramatic entrance on a safety wire, fell from the rafters and landed headfirst on a turnbuckle. He was rushed to a hospital—while the show went on—where he was pronounced dead. Bret has always maintained that the stunt would never have happened had he still been with the company, that Owen would have been in better storylines and would not have been subjected to such off-the-wall publicity stunts if he'd been around.

Part Four:
Writing with Shadows (2000-present)

Bret finally retired in 1999 after getting a concussion in a match against Bill Goldberg. He was done with wrestling, but we didn't finally come together as a family as I'd always dreamed. Instead, Bret and I spent a lot of time apart and fought when we were together. When he had his stroke, he was on his way to sign our divorce papers.

Beans and I were headed out for a bike ride, but changed our minds and went back inside for tea. When we walked in, Dallas was on the phone with Bret. "Mom, it's Dad, he sounds drunk." I wasn't going to take the phone, but my intuition moved me towards the receiver.

"Yeah, what?" I said flatly.

"Jules, can you come get me?"

"Where are you?"

He couldn't really tell me, and I stopped feeling annoyed and started worrying. "I fell off my bike and I can't get up…Just come get me."

"Okay, but where?"

"I don't know."

"Are you okay?"

"I can't stand up."

I asked if he had broken his leg, he said he didn't think so. He was starting to sound tired and slur his speech. I started to panic. I tried once more to get him to tell me where he was. He just kept saying he was where we had read the book. I had no idea what he was talking about, and decided to just start driving towards the bike path he frequently rode on. Beans and I jumped in the car, and I had her call him back on my cell phone. "Dad, look for something so we can find you." Beans looked at me nervously. I felt my grip tighten on the wheel. "What yellow bus, is it on top of you?" As we were driving, I looked up at an overpass and saw a big yellow construction bin. Maybe Bret thought it was a bus? We parked the car on the grass and ran over to the shale bike path. There he was, just sitting on the grass as though he were taking a break. We rushed to his side. He looked up at us and said, "Help me up." One of his eyes was wide open while the other was closed, and his mouth was drooping. We tried picking him up, but I was shaking too much and he was dead weight. He started to get frustrated and mad, "I don't know what's wrong with my legs."

"We should get some help," I said.

"No, nothing is wrong," he replied.

Beans looked scared and whispered to me, "What's wrong with him Mom?"

"Bret, we need to get help," I pleaded with him.

"Fuck, no, just hold my bike, I'll pull myself up."

We held the bike and he tried to stand but didn't have the strength. A rollerblader came down the path and I asked him to go get more help. Bret was starting to get sleepy and I yelled at him to stay awake. He looked at me and said, "I fucked up Mom, I'm not going to be home for a few days." I took off his hat and started fanning his face with it. Two girls came by and asked if everything was okay. One of them was a nurse, she told us it looked like he had a stroke. It felt like the ambulance was taking an eternity to get there. When the paramedics finally arrived, they checked his vital signs, put him on a stretcher and took him to the hospital.

I called Jade, Blade and Dallas and told them to meet me at the hospital. When I got there I went to Bret's room and saw him lying there, looking more vulnerable than I had ever seen him. I laid my head on his chest and tried not to cry. The children arrived and filed into the room. Blade rushed to his side, put his small hand on Bret's chest and said weakly, "Hey Pops."

"Boy, don't worry, I'll be out of here soon."

The doctors asked us to leave so that they could run some tests. One of them pulled me aside to ask about Bret's medical history. I told him everything I could remember before he cut to the chase, "Did he use steroids? Drugs?" I gave him what I could without saying too much.

We sat in the waiting room until they had finished their tests. When we went back into his room, Bret was barely conscious; they had sedated him while he was in the scanner because he kept moving around. The nurse told me to keep him awake, "It's important that he not fall asleep. Slap him as hard as you can on the chest, or even his face, if you need to." I asked Blade to help me, thinking it would help give him a sense of control over the scary situation, "If you've ever wanted to say that you've slapped your Dad around, here's your chance."

"Mama, is he going to be okay?" he asked, with tears filling his eyes.

"Yeah boy, you know your Dad."

I sent the kids home and stayed by Bret's side until they asked me to leave. I kissed Bret's face and chest and told him I loved him. "I know, Jules," he whispered sleepily.

Bret spent the following weeks in the hospital, despite his insistence that he'd be out of there in a couple of days. I was there with him every day. I would rush there in the mornings to help him go to the washroom; he had such pride, he wouldn't let the nurses help him. I would feed him, shower him and get him dressed for physiotherapy. I would massage his arms and legs, helping improve blood flow to his weakened left side.

Bret began to feel depressed over his newfound frailty, especially when he struggled with his physiotherapy. The stroke changed him in many ways, he was much moodier and more forgetful. Some things stayed the same, he continued with his secretive behaviour, refusing to take calls in front of me and lying about where he was. I kept my distance, not wanting to upset him. He would tell me it wasn't me, it was him.

One night as we lay in bed, Bret said there was something he wanted to tell me, "Jules sometimes I think I had the stroke because of all the terrible things I did. Did you know that on the day I went for that bike ride, I was on my way to sign our divorce papers? I was so fed up with where we weren't going anymore. And all we ever seemed to do was fight. I was firing you and my manager that day. I just couldn't do it with either of you anymore, you both had to go." I lay in silence, with my head on his chest. "Julie, I believe that accident was God's way of —" He didn't finish, I knew what he meant. We held each other tightly until we fell asleep.

We spent Easter as a family. Bret acted upbeat, but I could tell that something was wrong. I asked him what he wanted. "I don't know anymore," he said slowly. The next morning, I was in the bathroom and glanced over at a pile of reading material he kept by the toilet. There were some emails sitting on top—he'd been printing them out since the stroke, it made them easier to read. I read them. Now I knew what was up.

I was electrified, I couldn't stop reading what this girl had written. It was from a girl he had met in Italy and it was quite suggestive. I read it over to make sure I wasn't blowing things out of proportion, and then got angry at myself for allowing Bret to use me.

I was hesitant to confront him about it because I knew he would just deny everything. The first thing I said to him was, "Bret, please don't lie to me."

"About what?"

"I found something in your bathroom and I want the truth. I found an email from some girl in Italy, are you seeing someone?" I felt like a small child, about to be shipped off again.

"What? No."

"Bret, please don't lie."

"I'm not. What email are you talking about? Let me see it. What are you doing reading my personal email?"

"It was in the bathroom. Are you seeing anyone?"

"Why are you doing this again? I told if I met anyone I would tell you."

"I think you lying," I said sadly, "I'm leaving."

"It's not what you think. I met these girls while I was in Italy with Blade last fall and we've been emailing harmlessly. I told them I'd be back around for an autograph session, and they offered to take me around and show me some of the history."

I left, saying I needed time to think. Once again, it seemed like Bret was making his escape. He called me that night, again insisting that nothing was going on and that I was making a big deal out of nothing. I fell for it. Compared to the phone number written on hotel stationary I'd found a few years ago, it seemed relatively innocent.

Father's Day was coming up, so I took the kids shopping for presents. I wanted to make it a special day for him, because he was leaving on a promotional tour the next day. He said he was going to England or Amsterdam, he wasn't sure which one yet. We got him some new clothes for his trip and I picked up his favorite pie, key lime. I also wrote him a letter, telling him how much I loved him.

During his Father's Day dinner, Bret kept getting up and leaving the room to do something, or call someone. We went to bed early and tried to have sex, but he couldn't. I asked what was wrong, and he said he was tried. We were lying still in the dark, when suddenly he said, "Jul's no matter what happens I will always love you." It sounded like a goodbye.

The next morning, Bret woke up early to do some last minute packing while I waited to drive him to the airport. I was grabbing some of his bags to take them to the car, when I noticed his ticket lying on the floor. On it, in big black Sharpie, was written "ITALY." I stood frozen, staring at it. Bret came into the room, and I said "Don't lie to me, where are you going." He saw the ticket and lied anyway, "I don't know I think I start in England." I walked out and got into my car. I sat there, with my head on the steering wheel. I was going to drive away when he came out and put his stuff in the car. I decided to drive him to the airport anyway, I wanted to get rid of him, to make sure he got on the plane. We drove in tense silence, until he leaned over, touched my arm and said, "Julie it's not what you think." I pulled my arm away and said as viciously as I could, "Don't touch me." When we pulled up to the airport, I screeched to a halt and told him to get the fuck out of my car.

I didn't know what to do with myself and started smoking like crazy. When I got home I immediately told Jade all about it, sounding as though I had just witnessed some horrific accident and was still trying to process it. Dallas heard and told me to shut up about it. "We're sick of hearing about him and you," he explained. I was shocked, but understood why he reacted like that.

I would eventually find out that Bret had gone to meet Cinzia Rota, a woman he had met at an autograph session in Italy. She had shown up with the intention of marrying the Hitman. She'd been in love with him since seeing him wrestle as a little girl. Apparently, her entire bedroom had been plastered with posters of Bret, including pictures of him with the kids. This girl was everything Bret needed to feel like the Hitman again.

When he returned to Calgary, he tried to downplay the affair, claiming all they did was go sightseeing. I didn't believe any of it. He tried to get close to me again. He would reach for my hand when he spoke to me and refer to me as "Mom," implying we were a family again. I guess Italy hadn't gone as he had hoped. I told him I needed some space and went back home to Regina to figure things out.

He called me in Regina and his tone had changed. Suddenly he wanted to talk about how I'd never been there for him. He complained about how I didn't take care of him after he'd gotten his wisdom teeth removed, I guess he'd forgotten about the stroke. A few days later it was another call, and another change of heart. His voice was softer and he spoke about the old days. He had me laughing and remembering stories about old wrestlers. "We sure have been through a lot Julie, and I want to thank you for always being there for me," he said. "I can come home soon," I responded. He told me he had to go, and that he'd call back later.

He called back around ten thirty, ready with a speech: "I have been thinking a lot lately and I realize that you are never going to change, you will always be ragging on me for something and this past week I also came to the conclusion that all we have had in the past five years was sex and cooking."

"What are you talking about? Cooking?"

"That's all we have in common anymore. You cook, we have sex, that's it."

I laughed at the way he had summed me up and said, "Well, what are you going to do then?"

"I think we should end it and stop dragging each other down," he said, sounding relieved.

"Okay, do what you like, but don't call me when you're lonely."

I hung up and sat in the dark, hoping Mom hadn't heard our conversation. The next morning, after a restless sleep, I went to check my email. There was a message from Bret: "Dear Julie, I have met someone and I really like her. I am sorry I don't want to hurt you anymore. Love Bret." So he had made his decision.

I stayed in Regina for a while and devoted myself to writing in my journal and learning about my family history. I became obsessed with uncovering my family's past, thinking it might give me some insight into my life today. I was witnessing history repeating itself as I watched the kids struggle to adapt to their unstable family situation. Jade had the hardest time accepting Cinzia, who was only a year older than her. She told Bret she would give Cinzia a chance, but only if he'd shake hands and promise not to have kids with her. I was a little puzzled by her bargain, but then remembered how badly I'd reacted to having a step-family.

Things weren't any easier for Blade, who had been living with Bret while I was in Regina. They got into a huge fight. Apparently Bret freaked out at Blade and screamed, "If you ask me to pick her over you, I will pick her, and if you don't like it you can get the fuck out." Blade called me right after, asking me to get him out of there. I wasn't ready to go back to Calgary, but he continued pleading with me, so I told him I'd fly him out to Regina to stay with my family and me. When he arrived, I tried to be reassuring, telling him, "Don't worry about what the Hitman says to you, it's coming from his broken mind. No matter what, your Dad does love you. I will never stop loving you."

I went back to Calgary and bought a new house for me and the kids to live in. We had been living in a cramped condo and I wanted a nice home that my grandchildren would one day play in. I found a wonderful house near a beautiful pond and put a down payment on it immediately. And I mean immediately—before even going inside or contacting my financial advisor. It just looked so perfect. I started dreaming about my life there, surrounded by all the beautiful natural scenery and had to have it. The kids, too, got very excited and started arguing over who would get which room before they even knew how big they were.

A few weeks after we had moved in, Bret showed up at my door with a turkey and hit on me. I found it amusing and disturbing. I asked if Cinzia knew he was here. He said yes and that she didn't have a problem with us being friends. I let him in and showed him around my new house. We made small talk, but I tried to move things along quickly. My boundaries were stronger than they had ever been with him. He picked up on it and said he'd better go. I walked him to the door and before I could open it he said, "Julie, I still have strong cravings for you and it's been really hard to overcome them."

"You will," I said sympathetically.

I hugged him and shut the door, wondering what that was all about. I called Bret's assistant Marcy, who told me that Cinzia was in Italy. "Oh my God Julie, she leaves and on the same day he shows up with a turkey, looking for sex."

I found out about their marriage a few days later. They had been married for a while, but Bret had been keeping it a secret. He eventually gathered the kids together and told them. Blade came home right after, slamming the front door. I recognized the look on his face, it was the same one I had had so many times over the years. I asked him what was wrong, and he couldn't even speak, he was so mad. He took a piece of paper and scribbled: you better call Jade she will tell you. I said no, you tell me. He blurted out, "Dad married that girl!" I felt my stomach bottom out and my throat tighten.

Dallas came home and just started shaking his head when he saw me. I said to him, "I guess you heard, huh? I don't know what to say."

"Dad is a fucking idiot. Yeah, when he was walking out he just kept saying tell your mom, make sure you tell your mom." My heart was beyond shattered over his cruelty.

Perhaps the marriage had been too hasty. That winter Bret called to tell me that Cinzia had gone home, she was homesick and didn't like the cold. He was planning to split his time between Calgary and Italy. Hearing that made me want to run too, but where? Home. I booked a flight and told the kids I was going back to Regina to clear my head.

Next came what I like to call the Hall of Fame Screwjob. It was early 2006 and Bret was about to be inducted into the WWE Hall of Fame. I was thrilled, I knew how long Bret had been waiting for this. It had always been a dream of his to be included among the greats of the WWE, and it meant even more to him after the Montreal Screwjob and all of the dark times the Harts had gone through. It was a form of closure to him. I told Bret that I wanted to go, and that I would arrange it with Vince myself if I had to. He said he would take care of things for me, and invited me over for dinner.

I walked into Bret's house excited to see him and gave him a hug. Things we still uncomfortable between us, but we acted as though everything was fine. As I watched him baste tiny Cornish hens with orange sauce, I was reminded of when we used to get rid of the kids for the day to be alone and cook together, lounging in our own world designed for two. I wondered if he had chosen this specific meal, knowing it would remind me of the old days. I noticed a picture of his new wife on the wall and the reality of our situation came crashing back. How could he have me sitting in his kitchen, while his wife's eyes watched us eat the meal he prepared. I tried to contain the emotions I was feeling and found myself guzzling the expensive wine he had bought. I became chatty and nervous and couldn't wait to leave.

I left after dinner, but not before reminding him of his promise that I could attend the Hall of Fame ceremony. He said, "If anyone deserves to be there it is you. I will make sure you get the royal treatment." He walked me out to my car and we said goodbye. I wanted to kiss him on the lips, but decided to just give him a hug instead. I pulled him in tight and told him to take care.

The wrestling forums were going crazy with the news that Bret would be inducted into the Hall of Fame. Even I was receiving emails from fans and being asked to do interviews. I decided to do an online interview about what it meant to me and mentioned that I would be in Chicago for the ceremony.

Bret called to ask if I was all set to go. I said of course and told him that I'd really been looking forward to it. He asked me to be discreet while I was there. I started laughing, wondering how I was going to do that. "I'm not sure that when I walk in with the kids, I won't be recognized. If you're Mickey Mouse, I'm certainly Minnie." I thought maybe he just wanted me to stay out of the way of him and his wife. I had no intention of sitting up front or anywhere near her. I told Bret I would just hang back in the audience. Wanting to ease the tension, I suggested we all get together for Jade's birthday the night we got in.

"Bring Cinzia along," I said, "it might be a good thing for us all to see each other."

"We'll see," he replied.

A little while later I picked up the phone to an irate Bret, asking "What the fuck are you doing? Why would you post on the internet that you were going for fuck's sake! You're causing me all sorts of trouble right now. Why the fuck would my ex-wife be going to this?"

"What are you talking about, you set the whole trip up, you moron!"

"I told you to be discreet and not say anything to anybody."

I suddenly realized why he wanted me to be discreet: he hadn't told his wife I would be there. I lost my patience with the absurdity of the phone call and yelled, "Maybe if you had been honest with both of us from the start, this wouldn't be happening right now! I'm not so full of myself that I'd put my face where it would make others uncomfortable."

"Well you can't go now, if you do, I could get divorced. She made it quite clear that if you went, we were over." Bret said, his voice anxious and aggravated.

"So you don't want me to go then."

"No."

"Fine, don't worry, I won't come. But you can go fuck yourself. Maybe you should start telling the truth."

My heart was broken. In some weird way, it felt like I was being prevented from seeing the wedding of one my children. It was a fulfillment of everything the two of us had worked so hard for and dreamt about and I wasn't allowed to see it. It was like all of my sacrifices and support had meant nothing. Maybe I was overreacting, but at the same time I knew in my heart that Bret wanted me to be there; we had discussed this night for years. I chalked it up to the politics of marriage and resigned myself to being sidelined.

I didn't watch the ceremony, but knew when my phone started ringing like crazy that it had gone badly. I didn't want to answer it. Bad news is coming the ring seemed to say. Worried that something may have happened to the kids, I finally picked it up. It was a friend calling to ask if I had seen the speech. "Nope, didn't watch it, didn't care to."

"Okay, good. He publicly humiliated himself and your children. It was worst thing I have ever heard from him. "

"Now what did he do?" I asked as my stomach did flip-flops.

"Julie, I don't want to hurt you," she paused. "His whole speech was…All he talked about was his new wife, and how she was here for him after his stroke and took care of him. He called her his angel over and over again. He only mentioned two of the kids and didn't thank anyone else. The kids were all shaking their heads as he spoke. I'm so sorry to tell you that."

It was the worst betrayal of all. He may as well have body slammed me and spit in my face, it would have felt the same. The messages I got from friends and fans all told the same story. Those who knew our history were shocked at how he completely disregarded everything we had been through, shared, and survived.

Around the fall of 2008 I realized that my money had dwindled to a trickle. I had been in denial about it for a while, and then chased the false hope of earning it back through a reality show. It didn't happen. I was lead down a path of lies, investing my own money in it like water, assuming it would flow back in. I took money out against my house after falling into the belief that everything was a go, only to have it all crash down around me. I was facing bankruptcy and foreclosure. I was devastated and ashamed. Worst of all, I was proving Bret right.

I was about to find out who my true friends were. All the people who I had lent money to over the years—without ever really expecting it to be paid back – were nowhere to be found. Even some family members who I had helped out over the years were unwilling to return the favour. I found myself facing it all alone. As a last resort, I called Bret. He was still living in Italy on and off, but he was coming back to Calgary for a visit, so I asked him to meet with me. I hated the idea of letting him know how scared I was and knew he wouldn't be very sympathetic.

I'd say it took a lot of courage to face Bret with my problem. I was apprehensive about asking him for help and was starting to lose my nerve when the doorbell rang. We shared an uncomfortable hug and I invited him in for coffee. He gave me a weary glance, but came inside. We talked a little about the kids before our conversation fell into silence.

"So you're probably wondering why I asked you here?" I barely whispered.

"Yeah, what's going on?" His hands flew immediately behind his head. God how I hated that mannerism, it always made me feel inferior. We were both wearing baseball caps to avoid direct eye contact with each other, and I nervously tugged at my brim to make sure he couldn't see the worry splayed across my face.

"Bret, I need to borrow some money until I get my house sold. Otherwise I have to claim bankruptcy and walk away with nothing. I need to borrow enough for the three mortgage payments I missed."

"How will I get it back?" he said, with hint of pleasure in his voice. "What if you don't sell the house? What kind of money are you talking about? I don't have that kind of money lying around. What did you do with the money I gave you? Julie, you squandered it on the kids and God knows who else. I took a lot of backdrops for that money over the years."

"Look I promise to pay it back as soon as the house sells. It's nine thousand dollars. I wouldn't ask, but you did say you would never let anything happen to me. I'll let you think about it and get back to me, okay?"

"I can't. I got all this other stuff going on and I don't have the money right now. You should rent the house out. Maybe get the kids to pay rent or something."

I stood up and said I had a meeting to go to, but really I just wanted him to leave. I hugged him goodbye and told him that if things didn't work out for me, the kids would need a place to stay. His response was too cruel to repeat in writing.

I knew in all honesty that Bret didn't owe me a thing. That was a truth I accepted before I even asked to borrow the money. I had gotten myself into this mess, and was the only one to blame for it. I felt like I had let the kids down, which upset me more than anything else. I moved into a little place with Beans and split the expenses with her. I was living below the poverty line, but had too much pride to become a welfare case. When my sister called to offer me a job at the middle school, I took it without hesitation. I would be working as a janitor for $14 an hour.

I remember pulling up to the school in my Lexus and chuckling at absurdity of situation. I was almost embarrassed, and thought maybe I'd just tell them I wanted to help out and loved cleaning. I felt better when I met my boss Pat Dodsley, who was incredibly kind and sweet, and is still to this day one of my biggest supporters. The first couple of weeks were the toughest. It was a physically demanding job and I often came home with a sore back and my hands red from all the washing.

I kept going with the support of a few close friends and the wonderful school community, and eventually worked my way to financial independence. I sold my old Lexus to Beans, and became the proud owner of a 1999 Sunfire. It was the first car I'd bought on my own. I quickly stopped feeling ashamed at work; I was respected there and treated like I was part of a family.

My best friend Colleen Schimdt was always in my corner, cheering me on. Sometimes we take our friends for granted, but I never have with my soul sister. One day, after breaking down in tears in front of her, she gave me some words of encouragement I have never forgotten: "Julia, I am so proud of you and everything you've been through. Never once have you complained or said you couldn't do it. You picked yourself up and carried on. Every story you have ever told me is a story of sacrifice and survival. I am so proud to call you a friend. Your kids love you and everyone you meet loves you. I see for myself what you add to a person's life when they know you. Times are hard, but I know these tests will show you what you are made of. Fret not dear friend, someday you will look back at all of this and laugh at the naysayers!"

When my father died in 2012, I wrote him a letter and stuck it inside a burial box I made for him. In the letter, I promised to make him proud. I wrote that I will always be grateful for the things I have and hold my head up no matter what. I will always be Julie Smadu, the daughter of Stan Smadu and Margaret Lapierre.

Now I'm stronger than I've ever been. I don't worry as much about where my life is going. I figure I've already lived through so much and have ended up alright. Any failures I have faced have forced me to concentrate on the things that matter most, my friends and family. Their love has taught me who I really am.

My main concern right now is just trying to find enough time to spend with Jade's little girl, Kyra Beans. She is so much like Jade, sometimes I feel like I am raising Jade all over again. I rush over whenever Jade beckons me to babysit. When I walk in Kyra rushes straight for me and hugs me tightly. She even calls me Mom, which I find too endearing to correct. I like to think it's because I've helped raise her, but maybe it's because she always hears Jade calling me Mom, and figures it's my name. I look forward to taking Kyra wherever she wants to go. My kids have seen the world and have been around some incredible characters, and I'd love to be able to give Kyra similar opportunities.

Of course, Kyra won't grow up in the same world my kids did. These days Bret travels alone, or with his wife, and rarely invite the kids along. I understand why, and I realize the kids are older now, but it's still painful to see the family unity gone. Bret has drifted away from the kids, which makes me sad for them, even if they act like they are okay with it. Bret and I barely speak. I feel like I have nothing left to say to him. We certainly aren't drinking coffee and laughing about the old days.

I am grateful for every minute I have with my loving, funny children. I always tried to make sure my kids stayed grounded and I think it has paid off. They are all so caring and don't have a cruel bone in their bodies.

Jade has become such a wise, beautiful woman, who always impresses me with her gentle ways. In addition to being an amazing mother, she is also incredibly talented. She has recently started to design her own line of kimonos, which are quite magnificent. All because when she was a child, Bret and Tom brought these beautifully embroidered kimonos back from Japan for Michelle and me. For a while, they were all we ever wore and she had always loved them.

Dallas will always be my "Bear." I never imagined that he would become the leader of the five of us. If Jade, Beans and Blade are bickering, one of them will call Dallas to sort things out. He is the quietest of the kids, and approaches everything with logic and patience. He is also the most adventurous, often to my terror. Whenever I took him snowboarding as a kid, he would always sneak off to the most dangerous runs against my wishes.

I'd be waiting at the bottom, nervously eyeing the hills for him. Suddenly I'd get a face full of spraying snow, and see Dallas smiling right in front of me. Today he is happily working in the oil industry, and still snowboarding and rafting down the Bow River whenever he can.

Beans is the most loyal, loving person in our family. She is also passionate and focused, once she puts her mind to something, nothing can deter her. When she met her farm boy, Carter Kinvig, and decided to move to Saskatchewan to be with him, there was nothing we could do to keep her here. We love Carter like he is one of our own, but we had a hard time adjusting to Beans being gone. I missed her laughter and hearing her sing. Beans and I share the same love of music. Beans has always reminded me of myself when I was younger.

Blade always lights up my day. He is funny, affectionate and sensitive, while also being strong and resilient. He is in touch with his emotions and never holds back when expressing himself. Nor does he shut down anyone else when they are trying to express themselves. He too has been working in the oil industry, at the same company as Dallas. He has also been training to be a wrestler with Lance Storm. A few years ago, I hated the idea of my boys pursuing wrestling. I didn't want them to sell their souls, the way Bret did. I didn't want wrestling to be that mistress they would leave their homes for. But now I understand it's in their blood, and I of course want to support them in anything they choose to do. Blade is also very different from Bret, and I believe he would approach that world in his own way. Probably the sweetest thing he has ever said to me was, "Ma, I'm going to make sure I call you every day for the rest of my life. Did you know John Lennon called his Mom every day? I made a promise to myself that I'd call my Ma, just so she knows I love her."

This is what I live for. I have four fantastic kids who remind me every day that my life has purpose. I may have lost a lot, but what I have can't be bought.

Part Five: *Hart Strings*

Throughout the years, the Hart family has come together over tragic losses. Some left us at the end of a full life, some in the prime of their life, and some at just the beginning. They are fondly remembered by all of us.

Matthew Annis, 1996

A child should never die before their parents, especially not this one. Matt, a Hart grandchild, was a quiet, big-brown-eyed boy who resembled an angel. He was very shy and courteous. When Matt was small his father, B.J., had carried him upon his shoulders like Matt was another one of his body parts. Matt would crawl up his father's body and perch himself like a little bird on its nest. It was always delightful to see B.J. carry his son around like that. Matt stuck to him like glue, even while he was asleep.

Matt was quite a hockey player. His father had flooded a piece of his property so that his family could have their own private skating rink. Matt played well and wasn't as big a daredevil as his brother Ted. The Hart grandchildren all played together as though they were their own little community. They all got along fairly well, considering how many of them there were. Everyone got along with Matt, he was the one who shared and didn't instigate any fights or teasing. Matt could be found watching wrestling in the kitchen with his uncles and grandfather. Matt also loved wrestling with his cousins in the ring Stu had in the backyard. All the Hart grandchildren would bounce off the springy ropes laughing and assigning each other tag team matches.

When Bret and I first heard that Matt was sick, we had thought he just had a really bad flu. Instead it turned out to be a deadly disease. Our initial reaction was to remain positive and believe he was going to make it. The first night at the hospital we sat with his mom Georgia and B.J. in quiet disbelief that he had suddenly gotten so sick. I will never forget the look of disbelief on Georgia's face and the fear so deeply entrenched in her eyes. Georgia tried very hard not to show how scared she was and so did B.J. I was so proud of the optimism and faith that she portrayed for the rest of us; it made me believe he was going to make it.

When Bret and I went in to see him I was shocked at how he looked. I thought to myself, surely this is not the same little boy, with eyes so big and a grin which melted your heart, that now lay so quietly in his bed. Matt remained up and down the first few days. Bret and I had planned a trip to Seattle and asked Georgia if we should still go. Georgia said Matt should be fine and she would call if there was any change.

Bret and I had just landed in Seattle and checked into our room when we got a call from his sister Alison. Matt had taken a turn for the worse. We went home on the first flight out. My heart was so heavy for Georgia as she wrung her hands nervously and kept straightening out his sheets. She would push his hair back with loving swipes of her shaky hand and kiss him on the forehead. She had placed a picture of Matt above his bed because she wanted everyone to see that that was the real Matt, not this little boy who was so bloated from all of the medical interventions. When Bret stood by him and whispered in his ear that he was there, the monitors attached to him went up with each word he said. Bret encouraged him to fight and said that he was right there with him. It was quite a sight to behold, watching the gauges rise every time Bret spoke to him. I stood by the bed remembering the happy times, from the moment his mother became pregnant, to when he would bounce with his cousins in the ring at Stu's. It was while remembering those times that my tears were uncontrollable.

A few days later, we were scheduled to go on a WWF cruise. Georgia said that we should go, for the sake of our kids. Bret and

I both felt like we were abandoning their family, but in the end we decided to go. We were at the airport, about to begin the second half of our vacation, when Bret was paged over the intercom. I knew instantly that something had happened. I watched as he walked to a phone, and then saw his body curl. I knew Matt had died. Bret was on the phone for a while, then looked my way and hung up. I walked towards him, and he just hugged me and said, "Matt's gone."

We waited a couple of days before telling the kids. We took them to the beach, and watched them laugh and play in the sand, as we worried about how we were going to tell them about their cousin. I was especially worried about telling Dallas, who had often played Matt's tag-team partner. Bret and I were so quiet and sombre, I'm amazed the children didn't detect that something was wrong. I just kept thinking about how devastated the whole family must be.

We told the kids on the last night of our vacation. I wish we had waited until we'd gotten home, because it made the journey an extremely emotional one. Upon our arrival home we went and saw the family. Georgia firmly believed that her angel had gone to heaven, and so did I. Matt was an angel who was in our lives for a brief thirteen years, and in those years he touched us all with his loving presence.

Helen Hart, 2001

I don't remember calling Helen by her name much, she was always Grammy to me. I loved her deeply. She taught me so much, without ever being critical or judgemental of my upbringing. Helen was approachable no matter what your lot in life. She was charming and witty, and always made every effort to get to know you.

My last real conversation with her, before she fell ill, was right after 9/11. She was devastated by the attacks. After all, she was a New Yorker, and she never let any of us forget it. I remember calling her to see how she was doing. She kept repeating, "How could they do this to us?" as though it had been a personal attack on her family.

Helen went with Georgia to visit her sister in the States. Soon after she returned, she went into diabetic shock and had to be taken to the hospital. I think that all of the losses she had experienced of late had finally caught up with her. The loss of Owen, in particular, was something she never recovered from.

Bret and I went to see her in the hospital after his brother Keith called and said she wasn't responding too well to treatment. I was shocked at how small she looked with all of the wires and things sticking in and out of her. Georgia was standing at the foot of the bed, rubbing Helen's feet. She covered them when she was done, saying how mad Helen would be if she knew we were looking at her feet.

She was barely conscious and on a ventilator. I took her hand and rubbed it and whispered in her ear that I loved her, and that we would be back tomorrow. Bret looked uncomfortable and said it was time for us to go. He asked Georgia to call if anything changed.

The next day our visit with Helen seemed more positive. She was off the ventilator and had spoken with some of the family. I had worn my Yankee hat and jersey to make her smile. Bret and I stood on the side of her bed, and she asked Bret very softly, "How is Coombs?" Coombs was Dallas's dog. I took her hand and said, "Hi, Grammy. I wore the Yankee gear for you." She smiled and then softly said, "I love you." My eyes filled with tears and I said, "I love you too." It was the last thing she ever said to me.

The following day, we got a call from Alison saying Helen had been put back on the ventilator, and that we should come see her. Bret thought Alison was being an alarmist, and said we'd go the next day. I wish he'd listened to her. That night we went to bed and both woke up at the same moment—a breeze flowed over us, as though someone had come into the room. "Jules, did you feel that?" Bret asked. Bret's mom had come to say goodbye. We got the call early in the morning that Helen had passed.

Stewart Edward Hart, 2003

Stu became frailer after the loss of Helen. Like Helen, it seemed that Stu had seen enough of the tragedy that loomed over his family. I think he saw Bret's stroke as another sign of his family's ill fate. He started getting sick more often, and with greater severity.

Still, we were all surprised when we heard that he had been admitted to the hospital, and was having difficulty breathing. Helen had always said that Stu was immortal, and in a way I think we all believed her. Bret and I drove up to the hospital to visit him. Stu looked out of place, I guess because of the image I had of him in my head. He looked helpless to a degree, but also annoyed that we were staring at him with concern. He tried to sit up when Bret walked into the room, as though to show him he wasn't that bad off. He was wearing an oxygen mask and would tug on it when he wanted to speak. He asked how the tough guy, Blade, was. I knew it pissed him off that he had to struggle with each breath. When I kissed him goodbye, he gave me his trademark wink. His feistiness left us in good spirits.

Unfortunately, Stu's condition got worse. We headed back to the hospital, full of dread. When we got there, we saw the whole family gathered around his bed. Ellie's daughter Jenny, who had so often taken care of Stu during his illnesses, was right beside him, wiping his forehead with her hands. Jenny adored Grampy, he adored her equally. She was so much like Ellie, always taking care of others.

Bret stepped out for a minute because a reporter friend wanted to talk with him. Jenny and I stood on either side of Stu and watched helplessly as he began to fade. The nurse came in and we asked how much longer. "Not much," she said. I put my hand on his chest, because it looked like he had stopped breathing. His chest slowly rose, but felt cold under my hand. I asked Jenny to call for Bret. I whispered into Stu's ear, "Go to Grammy, she's waiting for you. You don't want to stay here anymore …" Just as I finished saying that, Bret burst into the room. Jenny, Bret, and I stood there and watched as he took his last breaths, our faces close to his chest, as though we were watching a baby breathe. There were no sounds or gasps for air—he just closed up like a flower. It was the most beautiful and spiritual moment I have ever witnessed. The three of us stood there, not in shock, but moved deeply by what we had just witnessed. Stu had finally gone to meet his soulmate, his sons and grandson.

I wish I had spent more time with Stu during his final years. I still have so many unanswered questions about his life, about how he managed to keep everything together and stay so strong.

Bonus: *Hart Songs*

A Special Bret and Julie Playlist for the Ages

Twenty-five songs that have special memories for me

1. Rickie Lee Jones—"Chuck E's in Love" (1979)

When we first met, one of the first things Bret said to me was, "You look like Rickie Lee Jones, this really great singer." I'd never heard of her, so I went to a record store to find an album cover with her picture on it. Oddly, I really did look like her. Bret and I became huge fans of hers over the years. He would often pick love songs of hers for me to listen to while he was gone, I think in the hopes that I would stay in love and wait for him. How could I not—he was a hopeless romantic!

2. Joan Armatrading—"Love and Affection" (1976)

Bret loved Joan. So did I. We used to sleep with the windows open in his sweatbox of a bedroom, listening to her music, as a giant tree swayed outside. Her music made you feel romantic. Our future was set to Joan Armatrading's music. We made plans and spoke of our dreams in the dark, while her music played in the background.

3. Christopher Cross—"Ride Like the Wind" (1980)

When Bret and I reconnected in January 1980, this became one of his favourite songs. He would drive back and forth between Regina and Calgary to see me, and always feel depressed on his ride home. He once told me that he was on one of those drives when he realized he loved me.

4. The Rolling Stones—"Memory Motel" (1976)

We played the Stones a lot. Bret knew they were my favourite band. This song reminds me of visiting him, and then moving in with him, in 1980.

5. Poco—"Heart of the Night" (1979)

We both loved Poco. I think this band was the closet Bret came to liking country-influenced rock. We saw Poco live in this little theatre in Calgary when I was about eight months pregnant with Jade. I held his hand through the whole show. It took us back to when we first started flirting with each other.

6. Led Zeppelin—"In Through the Out Door" (1979)

Of course, this being a band of our generation, Bret and I loved playing this album a lot. When we played "All My Love," it was as a statement to each other. 1980 was when we were truly and madly in love. It was also when I felt Bret was most my equal.

7. The Eagles—"Wasted Time" (1976)

This song reminds me of our first serious breakup. I panicked when I realized Bret was serious about wanting kids someday – I had flatly refused to have them. I remember saying, "I don't want what happened to me, to happen to my kids. I don't want them to ever come from a broken home like I did." Bret said, "Well, I can't be with someone that doesn't want to get married or have kids. I'm not your mom. I'll never leave you." Maybe I should have listened to my gut!

8. Cat Stevens—"Hard Headed Woman" (1970)

Bret loved Cat Stevens, and used to play this song a lot because it reminded him of me. It's your way or no way, he used to tell me. Sometimes I think Bret loved taking a little direction from a woman. He wasn't as tough as he made out himself to be. He was a vulnerable soul, even back then.

9. Peter Gabriel—"Solsbury Hill" (1977)

Bret loved Peter Gabriel, especially this song. It was one of his favourites.

10. Peter Gabriel—"In Your Eyes" (1986)

When he first played me this song he said, "Finally, someone has written a real song about your eyes, Vern (a nickname he had given me years before, among many others). This is about you, to me."

11. Elton John—"Rocket Man" (1972)

Elton John played a concert in Calgary just after Dallas was born. I didn't want to go, and said that I needed to take care of our newborn baby. We hadn't been getting along very well, and he was hurt that I didn't come. He said when Elton sang "Rocket Man," it was as if he knew what was happening in Bret's life.

12. Dire Straits—"Romeo and Juliet" (1981)

I choked up to this song when Bret first played it for me. If ever there was a song about us, or me specifically, this was it. I remember him quoting it to me in South Africa. I even bought him a star because of it.

13. Foreigner—"Waiting for a Girl Like You" (1981)

In the late 80s, Bret came home off the road with a surprise for me. He told me to stay downstairs, he would call me up when he was ready. He gave me the all clear, and as I walked up the stairs, he put this song on. He met me at the top of the stairs, took my hand, and told me to close my eyes and not open them until he said "okay." When I opened them, there was a painting of me with Michelle as teenagers. It was based on a photograph a friend of ours had taken. Bret had had it painted by an artist in the States. He'd laid a flower on top of the painting. I was so touched by his gesture of love and sensitivity—it was beyond belief.

14. Robbie Robertson—"Broken Arrow" (1987)

Bret had just bought a new Lincoln Continental and was blaring this song for me as we drove up to Stu's for dinner. When the line, "I'm gonna hold you in these arms of steel," came up, he turned the volume down and said, "That's me, Jules. Who else is gonna protect you?"

15. U2—"With or Without You: (1987)

Bret played this song a lot. He'd blare it in the basement while playing pool—sometimes by himself, playing this game he'd made up called Cowboys and Indians, which didn't need a second player.

16. U2—"In God's Country" (1987)

This song reminds me of driving to Tombstone with Bret to see the Old West. He pulled over on the highway and got out of the car to pick me a desert rose.

17. Bruce Springsteen—"Secret Garden" (1995)

I was depressed and my marriage was moving in a downward spiral. Bret was calling me "Crabby," an affectionate name of sorts, because of my moods. He played this for me when we were lying down, and all I did was cry. He said that ever since I told him about my childhood, he couldn't help but feel he had to protect me. My life had always been a secret garden to him, he said.

18. The Eagles—Take It to the Limit (1975)

This song was an old favourite of ours that we rediscovered together. We were in San Antonio, in a cozy little bar, when this song came on. Bret took my beer coaster and got up to borrow a pen from the bartender. On the coaster, he wrote: "If it all fell to pieces tomorrow, would you still be mine?" He made check boxes for yes, no, and maybe. Of course, I checked yes. He always made my heart melt when he did romantic things like that. That's the Bret I knew and loved.

19. Annie Lennox—"No More I Love You's" (1986)

This song spoke to me in a way that was hard to define. I didn't feel like it was about me, or Bret, or anyone else, but rather something that was missing inside me.

20. Sting—"Fields of Gold" (1993)

Bret loved this song. It was the same old mushy stuff of Bret holding my hand and listening to this while driving, or in the pool at our house.

21. Chris Whitley—"Poison Girl" (1992)

Bret said this song reminded him of me. Really? Sometimes I was offended by the songs he linked me with, no matter how good the songs were. I often thought he was taking pot shots at me. I'm still not sure if he thought I was poison!

22. Celine Dion—"My Heart Will Go On" (Theme from Titanic) (1997)

This song foreshadowed the end of my relationship with Bret. But it also joyfully reminds me of when Beans would sing it to us all.

23. Pearl Jam—"Nothingman" (1994)

This song had a greater impact on me when it was re-released in 2004. Bret and I had come to a definite end. Or so I thought. I played this over and over that summer as I struggled with Bret moving on. He remarried that fall.

24. David Gray—"Sail Away" (2001)

This was one of the last albums Bret played for me. We were in Hawaii with the kids the year he had his stroke, and he played it over and over. We all got pretty sick of it, but I now wish I had paid more attention to what he was trying to tell me through this songs.

25. The Clash—"Should I Stay or Should I Go?" (1982)

Bret loved The Clash. This was our wedding song. Should have paid more attention to the lyrics!

Acknowledgments

Thank you, Bret, for showing me a world that wouldn't have existed without you. I am grateful for all of the experiences we shared.

The Stu and Helen Hart family: I would like to thank every member of the family for always being so kind to me. I love each and every one of you.

My children: Jade, Dallas, Beans, and Blade. Thank you for standing beside me, behind me, and continuing to walk forward with me. I love being your mom! I am blessed with having such beautiful, intelligent, and gifted children. I am crazy in love with the four of you.

My Granddaughter Kyra Beans, the light of my life! My world is so perfect with you in it! The prettiest little baby in the whole world. I love you madly!

My brother Mark. I dedicated this book to him, as I always felt our story had to be told, whether it was good or bad. Mark left us too soon, but never does a day go by when I don't think of him. This is for you, Mark. I love you.

Jeff Eisen. My "womb buddy." Thanks for putting up with me. Thank you for the many deep discussions over the years. Life isn't so crazy with you in it. Thank you for being my sister Michelle's "King." Love you, my "brutha."

My mom: thank you for being there during the hardest time of my life. For the many hours you sat in silence while I typed away writing this book. And for always keeping the coffeepot full. Your patience with me during my darkest moods will always be remembered, Mom. I love you. Your most endearing quality has been passed onto me, Mom: your strength. And your sense of humor!

Dr George and Dr Marlene Smadu, I hope you realize what you mean to Michelle and me. With your family in our lives, it's like our childhood memories of when we were with Grandma come alive. They are the most happiest memories we have. We love you, Uncle George, Aunt Marlene, Joachim, Talitha, and Zach!

My dad: I will always take care of Michelle. I know you're near when a faint wind brushes my cheek. Keep shining the way, Dad.

To my sisters Sandy, Elaine, Karen and Mellissa, thank you for filling up my days with laughter and joy.

To my brother Ronnie thank you for keeping the love of 70s music alive.

To my numerous nieces and nephews, thank you for letting me live vicariously through your eyes. Your dreams and accomplishments motivate and inspire me daily.

Lawrence and Liz Elles. Thank you for everything you did for Mark, Michelle, and me when we were kids. We will always remember your kindness. I love you both.

My Aunts, Donalda and Annette Lapierre. Two of the funniest aunties I've ever known. I have had so much fun with you over the years! I love you both madly!

The Warren and Rose Doenz Family. Thank you for Kyle! I love you all!

There are so many friends to thank. I wouldn't have made it this far without their support and encouragement. The most important friend being Ashid Bahl. Ashid, you picked me up and dusted me off when my life with Bret fell apart. I don't know what would have happened to me during that crisis without you. You were the reason my life turned around. You taught me the importance of giving selflessly, and that our true essence is in sharing and giving back to humanity. Thank you for the many trips around the world you have taken me on, and also for encouraging me to be a member of the For the Love of Children Society. I have learned from you, Ashid, that the even the smallest of gesture of giving a small toy or pencil can brighten the face of a child less fortunate. Thank you, Ashid, for helping me repair my broken heart. All of us still call you the "Pied Piper" of lost souls! Kavita Bahl. Thank you for putting up with my whimsical ways! You are the best cook in the world! I love you both!

Dr Irene and Joe Orgnero. Thank you for being like parents to me and treating me like a daughter. Irene, I will never forget your words, "Be gentle with you, Julie, and keep your feet moving." I love you both.

Dr Beth Hedva and Harold Finkleman. Thank you for the support over the years. Our world is better with you both in it!

Marc and Taylor Floyd. Thank you, Marc, for being in my life. Thank you for making me feel like your important sister! Taylor, someday I'm going to make it to Vancouver and make you my godchild for real! I love you both.

Kevin Tremblay. You are a valued friend, Kevin. Thank you for always being there and helping me with the kids all those years when Bret was on the road. It will always be remembered.

Darryl and Christine Blinn. You are two of the sweetest and kindest people. I treasure you both.

Anne Diggs. Thank you for helping me raise my babies when they were small, especially Beans. You will always have a place in our hearts. I love you.

Media friends. Kenai Andrews and Richard Boudreau. My best friend Ryan Doyle down in L.A. Love my three Amigo's!

Dalhousie Raiders. Mike Byers, Rory Maitland, Tyler and Karla Madsen, Gregg Farineau, Matt Herensperger, Riley Haugen, Arthur and Baron Lee, Ryan Aulin, Erin Befus, Sarah Wirchowsky, Holly Wallwork, Calyn, Kendal, and Emerson Boyco, John, Mark and Grace Inaba, Jordan March, Christine Shier, Josh Dorey and Amer Akbrown. Thank you for continuing to be in my life. I love each and every one of you like my own.

Barry Dorosz. Thank you for bringing me in from the cold! Your kindness will never be forgotten. Most importantly, thanks for keeping my picture of Wayne Gretzky in your safe!

Theresa Dorey. My Moo. Thanks for being my companion during all those hockey practices when our boys were small. You have always been a good friend, Theresa. I hope you know what you mean to me. Love you madly, babe.

Tena Frasier White. You have been an angel to me more times than I can count. I owe you more then you will ever know. Thank you for all the times I could rely on you. Love ya!

Miki Bentley. I adore you. Thank you for all of your support these last two years. Your advice and friendship have been invaluable. Love you and your cosmic vibe!

Colonel Tim. You are one of my dearest friends. You have never failed me when I needed advice or support. I love your enthusiasm for life and what friendship means to you. I am honored to be your friend. I love you.

Steven Luigi Gonzales. I am so proud of you and all the things you overcame. You inspire me to keep reaching for my dreams. Love ya!

Charlie Belhumeur. Thank you. If you hadn't been so snap happy back in the day, I wouldn't have the images of Michelle and me that I treasure today!

Pat Dodsley. Thank you for giving me a job when I desperately needed one after my bankruptcy. Most importantly, thank you for being like a father figure to me over the years. You helped me buy my first car. You gave me things that a lot of people don't have. Thank you for believing in me and trusting me enough to go above and beyond. I don't know what I would have done without you. I love you.

Colleen Schmidt. You are so very special to me. We had a crazy overseas experience together and made history in India! A little scary, but nonetheless memorable! I remain your friend forever and always. Love you, Coll.

Nathaniel G. Moore. I don't know how to thank you for everything you've done. You came into my life just when I was deciding to drop this book. If you hadn't asked me to follow you on Twitter none of this would have happened! A few conversations later and here we are! Thank you, N. I am forever indebted to you. You made this all possible. You are now the fifth Hart child!

Dean Wilkinson. My Dew. Thank you, Dean, for never picking sides and remaining friends with Bret and me despite everything. You will always be my favorite man/girl friend! Your humor has resided in my heart since the day I met you, thirty-three years ago. I love you.

Wanda, Cori, and Jeff Leblanc. I appreciate you and everything you have ever done for me. This life of ours has been beyond crazy. It's been a hell of a ride and someday we are going to do that big RV road trip we have always talked about. You are the epitome of a best friend. I love you.

Gloria and Carter Kinvig. Thanks Mama K! Bunny—take care of my chicken! Carter, thank you for moving back to the "Fort." Love you both.

Bronwyne, Marek, and Amaris Billington, Trey and Trinity Burbank— you make my heart soar! Your crazy aunt loves you all too!

Thank you to the staff and teachers at Calgary Arts Academy. Importantly- Dale Erickson, Kevin Loftus, Josh Van Beers, and especially Jo Ann Schiffner whose help was invaluable!

My sister Michelle, my number one fan in the making of this book. Without your love, guidance, and belief in me, it would have never come to fruition. For that I am eternally grateful. I am so proud of you, Michelle, especially for the things you've accomplished in your life. Your strength is amazing and I'm proud to call you my sister and my hero. We have been to hell and back and finally found heaven. It's time for us to enjoy our lives. I love you to infinity and beyond.

About the Author

Julie Hart is the proud mother of Dallas, Beans, Blade, and Jade (and the equally proud grandmother of Kyra). Julie lives in Calgary, Alberta, and served as the overseas coordinator and operations specialist for the For the Love of Children Society of Alberta. She appeared in the 1998 documentary *Wrestling with Shadows*, with her ex-husband, Bret Hart, and is a frequent contributor to wrestling radio shows and blogs.